# Julia Harn's Memories of Georgia's Ogeechee-Canoochee Backwoods

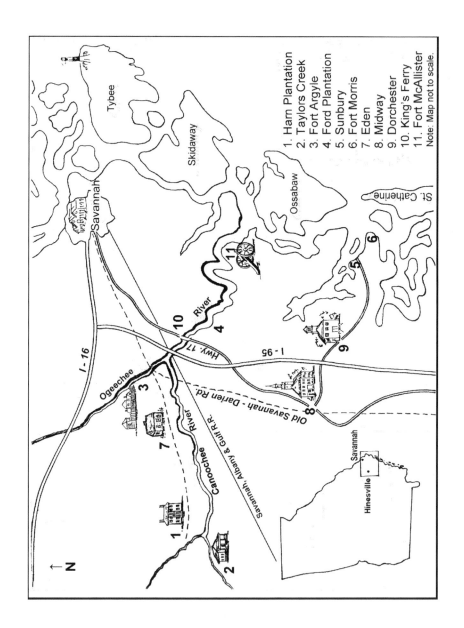

Ogeechee and Canoochee river environs.

Map adapted from Lucile Hodges Collection, Zach Henderson Library,
Georgia Southern University.

# Julia Harn's Memories of Georgia's Ogeechee-Canoochee Backwoods

## With Commentary on Savannah During the Civil War

Compiled by

Pharris Johnson

Julia Harn's Memories of Georgia's
Canoochee Backwoods

Compiled by Pharris Johnson

Library of Congress Control Number:
2015920131

ISBN: 0965854434
ISBN-13: 9780965854436

First Printing, 2016

Printed in the United States of America

Cover Design: Robin T. Poole

Front Cover Photo: Courtesy of Mary Ann
Peebles (Harn) Cofrin

# DEDICATION

To Dr. Curtis Hames, Jr.

My friend and collaborator

# CONTENTS

# PREFACE

Noted educator and author Julia Elizabeth Harn (1852-1941) wrote a series of vivid first-person accounts of life in the backwoods of the Ogeechee and Canoochee river areas of southeast Georgia immediately before, during and just after the Civil War. These memoirs are among the best available for this location and time.

The story of how Julia Harn came to write her backwoods stories is an interesting one. In her 70s during the late 1920s, while living in Gainesville, Florida, she wrote sketches of rural life for her own pleasure and that of her friends and family. Her working title for the memoirs was *Things I Remember* and was originally to be more of a personal story than historical. However, shortly after beginning the work, she changed the title to the *Old Canoochee-Ogeechee Chronicles,* and they took on more historical context. As she described in a 1930 letter, "As the story grew, . . . almost spontaneously, the better title suggested itself."

After reading a draft of her work in 1930, a cousin of Julia's took a copy to Mr. Thomas Gamble (1868-1945) of the Review Printing Company in Savannah, Georgia. Gamble was a publisher, historian and later, longtime mayor of Savannah. After reviewing the manuscript, Gamble responded with information about the potential of publishing the work as a book and the costs and process involved. He also suggested the content might be suitable for inclusion as a serial in the *Georgia Historical Quarterly.*

Mr. Gamble recommended that Julia contact Dr. E. Merton Coulter (1890-1981), head of the University of Georgia's history department and editor of the *Quarterly,* to learn of his possible interest in the material. Gamble, whose firm printed the *Quarterly,* also advised Julia that if published in this periodical, the type from the articles could be saved and re-printed in book form at greatly reduced cost.

Julia sent the manuscript to Dr. Coulter in early December of 1930 and in her enclosed letter asked for his assessment of its market value and potential for publication. Dr. Coulter replied that the material had merit and made suggestions to improve its suitability for the *Quarterly.* Dr. Coulter wanted her to add some Savannah material in her sketches, so she then included her observations of the city during the Civil War period. By September of 1931, the first installment of Julia's narrative was ready for publication.

The *Chronicles* were published from December 1931 to December 1932. They vividly portray the life, manners and customs of the people of Ogeechee and Canoochee river areas. Julia was very pleased with the articles in the *Quarterly*, but urged Dr. Coulter to insert some illustrations into later issues of the publication to increase reader interest. However, at that time the *Quarterly's* editorial style did not allow for an abundance of illustrations.

Already in her seventh decade when she wrote her stories, one of Julia's motivations for publishing was income. As she explained in a letter to Dr. Coulter in September of 1931, "I am in a very [financially] depressed condition. I have outlived family, home and financial resources, . . . and now earn my own living." At that time Julia ran Canoochee Lodge, a boarding house for students near the University of Florida campus.

Julia was previously a schoolteacher in Georgia and Florida and later lamented the low pay for public school teachers and nonexistent retirement benefits. However, her letters written during her later teaching period indicate she was nonetheless very fond of living in Florida because of the pleasant weather and love of her work. In a letter to Dr. Coulter she explained, "Many of the best years of my life were spent as a teacher in the public schools of Florida."

By 1934, Julia was still trying to find a book publisher for her *Chronicles*. She received rejection notices from publishers in Philadelphia and New York. Although they were complimentary of the work, the financial constraints of the 1930s Depression era undoubtedly forced publishing companies to be conservative. As one of her rejection letters explained, there was "great risk in publishing regional work from a little-known author." Even after these rejections, Julia continued to seek a publisher.

Julia persisted with her writing, and by 1937 had produced 15 more articles styled as the *Old Canoochee Backwoods Sketches*. Dr. Coulter published these in the *Quarterly* from March 1938 to September 1941, with the last two issues appearing after her death on May 21, 1941. In these sketches, she continued her true-to-life and entertaining descriptions of southeast Georgia folk life. As with her first articles, the time setting is around the third quarter of the nineteenth century in lower Bryan and Liberty counties. However, many of the backwoods customs and traditions she writes about are shared by other counties drained by the Canoochee and Ogeechee rivers.

During this period, she wrote newspaper articles on educational topics and gave talks as well. She also updated a play she had previously written, complete with Canoochee River-area dialect. Among her other pursuits were writing a supplementary reader for local schools, working in a clerical position with the Florida state legislature, and briefly managing a business school.

At 87 years of age, Julia still sought a royalty arrangement or sale of her manuscript. Fearing that the narrative by that time would be considered too old-fashioned, she wrote to Dr. Coulter seeking someone to edit the sketches and make them acceptable to present-day readers of the time.

Although Dr. Coulter was not able to find a book publisher for Julia's work and they never met in person, they maintained a warm friendship and regular communication for more than a decade. A year before her death in 1941, Julia wrote to Dr. Coulter and provided a colorful account of her 88th birthday celebration. Such was the esteem Dr. Coulter had for Julia, that it was he who placed a stone marker on her grave at Laurel Grove Cemetery in Savannah.

In 1977, Dr. Coulter described Julia as, "a wonderful writer and gracious lady of her times." He further noted,

> Years ago, sometime in the 1930s she wrote me, asking if I would be interested in publishing some sketches of the old Ogeechee-Canoochee country, in which she had written of her memories of the regions where she had lived as a girl. I wrote her to send some along, thinking that they might not be suitable for the *Quarterly*, but always willing to look at anything offered. I immediately saw the ease and grace with which she wrote, and I published all that she submitted at that time. A few years after that she offered a second group, and I published them.

The idea of publishing Julia's work in book form was revived after her death. Lucile Hodges (1906-1995) of Claxton, Georgia, learned of Julia's *Quarterly* articles in the late 1960s while researching historical information on Bryan County. Like Julia, Miss Hodges was a teacher and local historian. In 1964, Hodges published a widely acclaimed book, *A History of Our Locale, Mainly Evans County Georgia.*

Lucile became quite committed to editing and publishing Julia's articles. She visited Dr. Coulter in Athens, Georgia, in 1976 to discuss her idea. Dr. Coulter encouraged Lucile and gave her advice on the publication. During her visit, she presented Dr. Coulter with a liberal supply of Claxton Fruitcake, and he was delighted with her gift of Claxton's most famous product.

During Lucile's research, she contacted several of Julia's old acquaintances. Clara Olsen, a dean at Saint Leo College, gave the following background: "She [Julia] was eighty-seven years old, alert and known to me as an exceedingly excellent teacher of history. She had a dignity of bearing, a graciousness in receiving one, and the eyes of a woman exceedingly alert intellectually."

In 1972, Lucile wrote to a niece of Julia's in Gainesville, Florida, Mary Ann Cofrin, and told her of her intentions to publish an edited version of the articles. Mary Ann was supportive of the effort. Lucile prepared a draft manuscript including a preface; however, she did not find a publisher for the work, and it remained in manuscript form at the time of her death. In her notes for the unpublished book, Lucile summed up Julia's legacy thusly,

> From her rich store of childhood memories, from her scholarly background and profound sense of history, her love of family and pride of homeland, Miss Harn had the inspiration and ability that made her eminently qualified to write well of the life and times of her region.

Julia's writing did not go unnoticed in later times. Some of it was featured prominently in several publications in various forms, including the excellent Bryan County history book *From Beautiful Zion to Redbud Creek: A History of Bryan County.* The author, Buddy Sullivan, liberally quotes from Julia's writing and describes her work as "the best account of early life in the Cross Swamp-Barbeque Creek section of old Bryan County." He skillfully weaves Julia's first-person accounts into his narrative in an exceedingly interesting way to provide background and context. Julia's articles were also referenced extensively in *A Historical Archeological and Architectural Survey of the Fort Stewart Military Reservation,* published in 1983. Among other books and articles, her work is also cited in *Swamp Water and Wiregrass* by Georgia Southern University professors George A. Rogers and R. Frank Saunders, Jr., and *Taylors Creek – 1760-1986* by Wyman E. May et al. R. L. Cooper, a realtor for Henry Ford Plantation operations in Bryan County, used Julia's articles as source material for his *History of Bryan County, Georgia.*

Readers will find the articles in this publication as they were sequentially written and published in the *Quarterly.* Also, the appendix includes Harn family information written by Julia. There is some duplication in the articles, but the narrative is largely left intact as each of the serials includes supplemental information. Please note that Julia uses the actual names for her family and many public figures; however, some others have fictitious names. One can use their judgment as to which are in these respective categories. For example, she humorously refers to her Bird family neighbors in Taylors Creek as the "Birneys."

Readers will note Julia's frequent use of dashes in her narrative. When printed in the *Georgia Historical Quarterly*, the articles contained these elongated dashes as a stylistic feature, and they have been retained in this book.

Julia Harn was a Southern lady of her times. As such, her outlook on and descriptions of African-American slavery in her writing, although benevolent, are typical. Though she speaks of mutual respect and kindness regarding her family's relations with their slaves, some biases remain in her views.

The editor of this publication learned about Julia Harn's *Georgia Historical Quarterly* articles from Evans County, Georgia, resident and local historian Dorothy Simmons. After reading the articles, I too felt they had great importance. Upon reviewing Julia Harn's correspondence regarding the articles at the Georgia Historical Society in Savannah, her manuscripts in the University of Florida Library Special Collections in Gainesville, Florida, as well as information at Georgia Southern University's Zack Henderson Library about Lucile Hodges's attempt to publish an edited manuscript, I undertook publishing Julia's stories in this volume. I strongly believe the book is needed to ensure future generations full and easy access to Julia's fine work, and to honor her memory with her wished-for book at long last in print.

# ACKNOWLEDGMENTS

Special appreciation goes to a number of people and organizations that have contributed to this book. Mary Ann Peebles (Harn) Cofrin, Julia Harn's grandniece, of Gainesville, Florida, generously provided access to her information about Julia in addition to the photo used for the front cover. She also reviewed the book's front and back material. Mary Ann's father, Samuel Peebles Harn, was Julia's nephew, and he showed much devotion to his aunt. He was manager of the Gainesville Chamber of Commerce and the namesake of the University of Florida Samuel P. Harn Museum of Art, one of the largest university-affiliated art museums in the United States. Mary Ann's fine book, *Family Letters 1893-1933*, provides interesting correspondence between Samuel and his Aunt Julia.

The late Lucile Hodges' efforts to have Julia's work published are most laudable. Although she was unable to complete the project, she exhibited much initiative and determination. Lucile Hodges' papers in the Zack S. Henderson Special Collections at Georgia Southern University (GSU) were extremely helpful in understanding her endeavors to publish Julia's work. The frontispiece map in this book was adapted from a draft of a map included in her papers. Wendy Harrison, archives assistant at GSU, was especially kind in efficiently helping me access the Hodges Collection.

Many thanks go to the eminent Georgia historian, Buddy Sullivan, for his review of portions of this book's manuscript. His excellent use of Julia's historical accounts in his publication *From Beautiful Zion to Redbud Creek: A History of Bryan County* added immeasurably to that superb book's success. Readers are urged to refer to his book for additional information on the Harn family and Bryan County.

I am very thankful to the staff of the George A. Smathers Libraries at the University of Florida for assistance in reviewing their Harn files. Their professional approach made my research easier.

As always, I am indebted to my wife, Annie, and sister, Linda Hester, for their editorial support and thoughtful encouragement.

The Georgia Historical Society has published their *Quarterly* continuously since 1917. Had the publication's former editor, Dr. E. Merton Coulter, not included Julia Harn's work in the *Quarterly*, we likely would not have the opportunity to read it in book form now. Keep up the legacy of good work, Georgia Historical Society!

# BIOGRAPHICAL SKETCH OF
# JULIA HARN

Julia Harn's oldest American ancestors were a Scottish immigrant of colonial Georgia, John Harn (1710-1765), and his wife, Elizabeth Beddise (d. 1775). This first John Harn received a colonial land grant in 1748 on what became Dublin Plantation, later Richmond, and is now part of Richmond Hill, Georgia. The Dublin Plantation site is considered by many to afford one of the most beautiful views along the scenic Ogeechee River. This land later became integral to Henry Ford's Plantation when Ford established his winter home in Bryan County in the mid-1920s. As expressed by one observer, the first John Harn "was a man of vision and pride, trustworthy, religious, and fiercely loyal to Colonial Georgia." An early family sketch prepared by Julia is included in the appendix.[1]

Julia descended from colonial John's son, William Harn (1735-1816) and his wife Sophie Robinson (d. 1768). Next in Julia's line were Julia's grandparents, John Harn II (1784-1851) and Sarah Hayman (1790-1853). Their son, Samuel Harn (1826-1901), was Julia's father, and her mother, Julia Elizabeth Ellarbee (1829-1892), was the daughter of Jesse Ellarbee and Elizabeth Bragg Ellarbee.[2]

Born in Bryan County in 1852, Julia's first years were spent on her father's plantation. It was primarily a stock-raising enterprise, supplemented by timbering. Samuel Harn inherited this property from his father, John Harn II, as part of the elder's Belknap Plantation. Julia lived her early childhood on what she called the "Old Place," approximately one mile north of the Canoochee River near a bend of the river known as Harn's Cove. The plantation, located in the vicinity of the Hencart Road, was a few miles east of the Canoochee River Bridge of antebellum times. The road is part of present-day State Route 144, and on the Fort Stewart military reservation. Her maternal grandparents, Jesse and Elizabeth Ellarbee, lived nearby at the junction of the Canoochee River Bridge and county courthouse roads.[3]

In 1856, Samuel and his family moved from Belknap Plantation to a new location across the Canoochee River about five miles distant from Belknap. Julia recounted that her mother was the impetus for the move and convinced her husband to relocate to a new area with more neighbors and less of the monotony of plantation life. Samuel was in the mercantile business in his new community, and their new home was near the antebellum Canoochee River Bridge and not far from the Macedonia Church.[4]

In the late 1850s, Julia and her family moved to Taylors Creek in Liberty County, about six miles distant. This relocation gave the family's children an opportunity to attend the highly regarded Taylors Creek Union Academy. Incorporated by the General Assembly of Georgia in 1833, it became one of the most recognized schools in the state. Samuel continued his occupation as a merchant in Taylors Creek.[5]

Their stay in Taylors Creek was short-lived, as Julia and her family moved to Savannah in October of 1860. The relocation to Savannah proved auspicious as the Taylors Creek School, a major influence on their decision to live in Taylor Creek, temporarily closed due to the war's drain on manpower. After first moving to Savannah, Julia attended private school and, later, public schools during the war. She was an eyewitness to many Civil War activities in that city. From the vantage point of her family's house on the west end of Liberty Street, she recalled, "Many a night we went to the windows and watched company after company move down the parkway in semi-darkness to the beat of muffled drum, marching to the railway station." Her father was a purchasing agent for the Confederacy and travelled extensively across Georgia, Florida and other Southern states during the war, procuring provisions for the army. After the war and as a member of her school class from Chatham Academy, she visited Robert E. Lee on his last trip to the city in 1870.[6]

The family continued to live in Savannah for a number of years after the war. According to the Savannah City Directory, Julia's mother ran a boarding house, while her father was a butcher and then later a clerk. Julia attended several noted schools in Savannah and graduated from the highly rated Chatham Academy in 1870. Hired through a competitive interview and exam process, Julia started her teaching career in 1873 at Massie Common School in Savannah.[7]

In 1884, Julia and her family moved to Orange County, Florida. Julia's father was no stranger to Florida, as he had travelled the territory extensively in the course of his aforementioned duties there during the Civil War. Her father's move to Orange County was to enter the real estate business there during a period of land speculation. Prosperity had arrived in the area with the county's first railroad. However, the risks of his occupation were significant and as Julia reported later, they "lost everything" when the family's business failed. She taught school there for a number of years. After the financial setbacks in

Florida, she and her family returned to Savannah where she resumed her teaching career.[8]

Early in the second decade of the twentieth century, she moved back to Florida and taught in Florida public schools. Later, she leased a house, which she named Canoochee Lodge, near the University of Florida campus in Gainesville and rented rooms to students. She lived in Florida for the rest of her life and never married.[9]

She was still working at age 75, and as she said in a 1927 letter to a cousin, "I have not many more years to live and some of the things I have to do must be done shortly, perhaps very shortly." This sentiment was likely her wish to write the story of her early life. She accomplished this objective with style and grace over the next few years. However, she lived 14 more years after she wrote the prophetic letter of 1927.

She passed away in 1941 at the age of 89 from injuries sustained in a fall. It was her wish to be buried in her family plot in Savannah's Laurel Grove Cemetery, where she rests with many of her close kin.[10]

### Notes

1. For an excellent review of Julia Harn's family history see Buddy Sullivan, *From Beautiful Zion to Redbud Creek, A History of Bryan County, Georgia* (Darien: Darien Printing and Graphics, Inc., 2000), 149-151; J. Dixie Harn, *History of Bryan County 1793-1985*, (Bryan County Historical Society, 1985), 91.
2. Sullivan, 149-151; Julia E. Harn, "Old Canoochee-Ogeechee Chronicles" Georgia *Historical Quarterly* 15, (December, 1931), 346-348.
3. Harn, *GHQ,* 15, (December 1931), 346-348.
4. Ibid., 346-347; 16, (March 1932), 47; Department of the Army, A *Historical, Archeological, and Architectural Survey of the Fort Stewart Military Reservation Georgia*, 1983, 127-128, 133.
5. Harn, *GHQ,* 16, (September 1932), 233; Wyman E. May et al., *Taylors Creek, 1760-1986*, 79.
6. Harn, *GHQ,* 16 (December 1932), 233, 301-302, 307; Julia Harn letter to E. Merton Coulter, December 12, 1930, Georgia Historical Society, GHS-GHQ: Collection 1361-AD.; Chatham County Deed Book 3V, 65, 66.; Julia Harn letter, November 20, 1935, Vertical file "Harn," Georgia Archives.
7. Savannah City Directories 1871, 1874-75, and 1883, located at Georgia Historical Society; *Savannah Newspaper Digest* WPA Indexes for 1870 and 1873: *Savannah Morning News*, April 30, 1870, 373, and May 28, 1873, 404, located in Savannah Bull Street Library.
8. Julia Harn letter to Mary Mckinstry March 22, 1928, letter in possession of Mary Ann Peebles (Harn) Cofrin; Mary Ann Peebles (Harn) Cofrin, *Family Letters 1893-1922*, December 2000, frontispiece caption.
9. Julia Harn letter to Mary Mckinstry March 22, 1928; 1885 Florida Census, Orlando, Orange County; 1900 U.S. Census, Savannah, Chatham County.
10. Julia Harn Obituary, *Gainesville Daily Sun*, May 22, 1941.; Julia Harn letter to Mary Mckinstry July 27, 1927, letter in possession of Mary Ann Peebles (Harn) Cofrin.

# PART ONE

# OLD CANOOCHEE—OGEECHEE CHRONICLES

OLD CANOOCHEE—OGEECHEE CHRONICLES

By Julia E. Harn

In these Chronicles I have attempted to portray the domestic life of the people of certain quiet Southern communities in the period immediately preceding, during, and just after the War Between the States. The scenes are typical, the manners and customs true as they prevailed among the refined classes of plantations, small community, and city.

No attempt has been made to deal with the ultra rich nor with historic social functions, but with the life of the people in the quiet of their homes.

These are things I remember from my own life, side lights upon those old days. If these glimpses of that faraway time have any charm to stay the reader's attention, my purpose has been well served. These pages that follow, I dedicate to the memory of my mother.

# 1

## LIFE ON THE OLD PLANTATION—CANOOCHEE

It was a goodly land and fair to see, a lordly domain, extending for miles along one bank of a beautiful river with a weird old Indian name, Canoochee, and not far from where this river joins a larger river, the Ogeechee, on its way to the sea.

The location is in the far South in the state of Georgia. The land was heavily timbered with southern pine, live oak, magnolia, cherry, and shrubs of lesser growth; the soil was productive and yielded abundantly to cultivation. It was here that my Scottish ancestor, John Harn, came just before the middle of the eighteenth century bringing with him his family, consisting of a wife, nine sons and daughters, and about thirty indentured servants. The indentured servants were later succeeded by African slaves, while they themselves—or many of them—secured land and settled in the surrounding country, and thru the evolution of time became reputable and worthy citizens.

This colonial ancestor I am proud to relate (and the history of the period bears me out in the statement) took his rightful place in the conduct of governmental affairs; became an American patriot; his sons were in the Revolutionary War; his purse and home were open to the needs of any wounded Continental soldier. He hated the Tories, by whom he was largely encompassed, and from whose depredations upon his property he greatly suffered. This dislike of the Tories he transmitted to his children who, to the third generation, held in unreasoning contempt any whom they knew as having come from American "Troy" ancestry.

Agriculture, and stock raising on a somewhat extended scale, occupied the family through several generations and brought prosperity and happiness. There was no lordly wealth, but the realization of the prayer of Agar,—"Give me neither poverty nor riches." The slaves knew their master thru better acquaintance than mere identification by sight.

My Grandfather, the second John Harn of the American line, when master, was a man of affairs and knew much of what was going on in the outside world. News was slow in traveling across the land in the early nineteenth century, yet not so slow but that it became known when Andrew Jackson wanted reinforcements for his New Orleans campaign. Two sons of the family, brothers of my grandfather, at that time being eligible joined the army in the War of 1812. Fortunately they returned home alive, and not much the worse physically for their experience, and with their love of country greatly enhanced since they had helped to save it. That it was afterwards learned that the battle of New Orleans was needless, and would never have been fought if communication with England had been only a fraction—a very small fraction—as rapid then as now, mattered but little against the fact that "Old Hickory" had made a glorious fight and had settled for a long time any thought of further British foolishness against the wonderful young United States. The War of 1812 furnished material for fireside stories nearly as important in their bearing upon the family life as had the Revolution.

The interests of the family lay in their home and neighborhood life. The war cloud that began to gather in the North in the early nineteenth century was but faintly discernible; the slavery question had not yet taken definite shape; the relations of master and slave were smoothly peaceful. This ideal condition had prevailed thru many decades at the time when my father, a young man, brought my mother, a young woman, a bride to his home.

Here, amid very happy surroundings I, their first child, was born. That was a long time ago. I was but four years old when my mother, tiring of the monotony of plantation life and the scarcity of congenial neighbors, induced my father to leave the "Old Place" and take up our abode in a more populous section. Land then was held in large tracts for the very purpose, in many instances, of keeping out other settlers—a mistake, perhaps, since land like many other commodities is not valuable unless ownership is shared. This ancestral property remained in our family for many years afterwards, but we never returned to it as a home. Tho I was less than five years old, and never saw the old home after I was seven, I have an excellent memory (an inheritance perhaps from my father) and so vividly were the scenes of my young life impressed upon my mind and heart, that I can easily recall many incidents of that faraway time. Some dates and distances were learned in other ways, but the localities and happenings I remember distinctly.

The road from the river bridge, four miles away, led past the very old church and the churchyard where lay, in their last long sleep the dead and gone of four generations. It climbed the hill, passed the site of the family mansion which had been destroyed by fire some years before, and on past the home, the farm buildings and fields, beyond the bridge over the creek, and on then a great virgin forest to other settlements, the nearest of which was two miles or more away. The avenue from this "big road" led up to the home of my parents. It was the custom to set the dwelling house some distance back from the road that ran past, for the sake of greater privacy and seclusion.

Grandfather Harn had died the year before I was born. Grandmother, who survived him by two years, died from the results of burns received in the fire that destroyed the great house. The house in which I was born was a new log house erected just before the destruction of the larger home, but it was commodious and attractive in its beautiful simplicity and comfort. It contained a few pieces of handsome furniture that remained in the family for a long time—solid mahogany tables, four-poster beds with canopies, one or two large chests of drawers, a highboy standing well off the floor, with overhanging mirror. A large painting of the Madonna and Child (rescued from the fire) held a conspicuous position in the big entrance room known as the hall, and used as living and dining room in one. A heavy sideboard with some pieces of real silver had a place of honor in this room. There was a guest chamber with its high, white bed. Feather beds were popular in those days, along with canopy tops, valences, longfringed counterpanes, hand-woven coverlets and patchwork quilts, clean scrubbed floors, home-made rugs and cushions. There were big rocking chairs and a low, rush-bottom chair in which my mother sat when she rocked and sang the baby to sleep. I do not know what she sang then, but most likely it was "How Firm a Foundation," since it was a lifelong favorite of hers.

The chairs used on the long piazza were home-made. There was usually some man in the neighborhood who made chairs in goodly

numbers, but frequently they were made by an old slave Negro on the
home place, and very skillfully. The woodwork was mostly hickory, and
the seats of cowhide, cured so as to leave the hair on. Very attractive
and very comfortable too were those chairs, and made to last.

In passing, I would pay tribute to certain old slave men who were
proficient in fashioning baskets of various kinds for farm use. They
did most of this work at night and were allowed to have the money
they received for baskets sold. Every right-minded master paid his
slave for the baskets he himself used. There were strong baskets
made of white oak splints riven by hand, and baskets of grasses.

You may think I am drawing upon imagination while relating
these things, but I am not. It is all so clearly visualized in my mind
that I have but to close my eyes to see it all pass in review before me.
There was the orchard back of the house with the beehives under the
peach trees; the mustard and other vegetables sending up long straight
stems with yellow flowers at the top going to seed. One day I was
walking in the garden and was stung by a yellow jacket. I screamed
with pain and Old Maum Rhina, a black woman, came to my relief.
She took from her capacious pocket a piece of plug tobacco, pulled
off part of the brown leaf, which she moistened with her lips, wound
it around my finger and sent me to my mother to have the wound
tied up.

The old woman had been a slave in our family all her life and
was a famous cook. At my grandfather's death she had been given
her freedom but made her home with some of the family, who were
bound to take care of her. Moreover, she had the choice of the
children she would live with. My father being the youngest son and a
great favorite, she elected to live with us. In that particular part of the
Southern seaboard the old Negro women who were house servants,
and generally nurses, were not called "Mammy" but "Mauma" (as
spelled), or if the name was added it was shortened into "Maum," as
Maum Rhina. Maum Rhina had her little home, a log house down in
the quarters, where she raised chickens that were her very own. She
was permitted to take the children and nurse down to her little cabin.
We liked to go there and when we were old enough would even run
away to go to Maum Rhina's. Everybody, Negroes and whites alike,
respected her. She really was not required to do any work unless she
wished, but she was a very important member of the family, so to

speak, a woman of much energy. She was not decrepit, and must have enjoyed in a rightful way her position of much importance. She bossed things in the kitchen, held the young Negroes to their work, looked after the cream and butter making. The churning was done in a large barrel churn under a big tree in the back yard, the old woman directing the process, instructing—and occasionally scolding—some younger Negro. The buttermilk was poured off and set to cool in stone crocks; the butter washed and made into golden balls ready for use was placed in the cool shady dairy house to chill. In those days there were not so many conveniences as in these later times and housekeeping involved more labor. But labor was plentiful and cheap. Each household was a little community in itself, and people knew methods and adaptations that are not practiced now. If no convenient spring could be used in connection with the dairy, there was a deep well of very cold water, plenty of shade, an earthen floor in the house that was always cool, and plenty of shelves for the milk. The cream was ripened in large earthenware bowls. I remember those rows of bowls, and that they were yellow, like most of our mixing bowls now. In some homes, though not in mine, I have seen gourds used as receptacles for milk. Gourds were usually grown along the back fences of the gardens; they were of various shapes and sizes, some round with long handles were cured and used for drinking gourds, others, large and deep, were for various service, to take eggs to market, etc., or serve as milk containers, and some tiny ones for ornamental purposes. Old Maum Rhina kept some of her clothes in a very large gourd shoved under her bed. It was not poverty pure and simple that caused resort to such expediencies, but transportation was difficult and considerable ingenuity was needed to overcome this handicap.

Breech-loading guns were unknown at that time and hunters carried shot and powder for the muzzle-loading muskets and rifles. I have seen small gourds used for powder, but as a rule the powder container was a small horn, a cow horn. Horns used for blowing were sometimes very pretty; they were scraped and polished and hung by a cord around the neck of the hunter. We had a large conch shell for a dinner horn, but, as I remember, the sound from the polished cow horn was far more musical. My father and his friends were fond of hunting; everybody kept some hounds. My father was devoted to his pedigreed hounds and with pardonable pride would show the length of their ears and points as to form that indicated the thoroughbred. The baying of the hounds he thought the finest music in the world; and I assure you that when the horns were blown to call the dogs together for a hunting trip it was a truly exciting time. The neighbors would gather at one place, the horns were blown to announce each new arrival, the dogs would answer, and a regular orgy of noise and dancing would ensue.

Game of all kinds was plentiful—so plentiful that there was no restriction as to closed seasons. Anybody could hunt anywhere at any time without legal offense. The only restrictions were by a "gentleman's agreement" and sportsman's rules. These were rigidly observed. Deer, wild turkey, birds of all kinds in the woods and fields, wild ducks in season from the river, with fish at all times, made living abundant and easy and furnished sport for the men. Wonderful tales were told of bears in the river swamp, the proof of whose presence was found by getting a strong trap for the "varmint." A pen which was a trap was sometimes set for wild turkey, but it was usual to find the nesting place of the turkeys and go hunting for them in the early morning. The hunter would provide himself with the proper ammunition and a "gobbler." This was made from the large tusk of an alligator and when rightly managed would very cleverly imitate the call or gobble of the turkey. The hunter having arrived just before day at the place where the turkeys were in the river swamp, would stealthily and with great caution seat himself near, and just at the right time, when the turkeys were ready to leave their roosting limbs for the ground, would call, with his artificial "gobbler" a close imitation of the call of the birds. If he were a good shot he would probably secure what he wanted in the way of turkey for dinner. A good sportsman is never greedy, and there were, in that faraway time, certain rules governing the quantity of game one should take in one day.

I have mentioned the alligator. There were alligators in the river and even in the larger ponds. Nobody liked alligators. They seemed wicked beasts and were a menace to the hunting dogs. Alligators had a special fondness for dogs; the dog that swam the river after a deer was likely to be caught by them, and that was the last of the dog.

My father, tho American born, as was his father before him, was very Scotch in his ways. He held to old traditions. He loved the sound of bagpipes—where had he heard the sound of bagpipes? There were sometimes wandering minstrels who came to the plantation playing their bagpipes and, shabby as most of them were, they were made welcome in his father's time. Indeed, there was a house detached from the main dwelling, furnished with beds and simple furniture where strollers and travelers not quite acceptable as guests in the home were given food and shelter free during their sojourn. The bagpipe players, my father has told me, came and sometimes returned. Their coming was welcomed by everyone, especially the children and dogs. The bagpipes could be heard a long way off and as the first sound borne by the wind was heard at the home, the children, Negroes and dogs would start screaming with delight. The strollers were welcomed by the master as much for their nationality as for their music. Truly, "One touch of nature makes the whole world kin."

All kinds of livestock were raised on the place—horses, hogs, cattle, sheep and goats; there were chickens, turkeys, geese (kept for their feathers) and ducks—probably for the noise they made. I remember my terror of an old gander. When I saw him coming I would scream and run for protection. His hissing was certainly fierce. There was a poultry yard and a little yard just beyond in which the geese were kept, but sometimes they would escape into the back yard. A small creek crossed the road not far away and the geese would fly off to that in a long line, screaming as they went, plunge in and swim up and down in evident delight to themselves as well as to those who liked to watch them.

Perhaps the most wonderful thing about the old home was the great flower yard and my mother's flowers. On approaching from the avenue one was greeted with a wave of perfume, the combined fragrance of roses, honeysuckle and flowering shrubs. The roses were Mother's favorites. The high arch over the front gateway was covered with running roses. There were roses and roses—sold fashioned multiflora, spicy pink and red roses that bloomed in spring, fair white roses, and the ever-blooming kind that lent brightness to nearly every month in the year. In addition to roses there were pinks and syringa, hollyhocks and cape jasmine, and at the fall season chrysanthemums—not the gorgeous beauties we have now, but equally sweet and attractive, and just as sure a reminder of the cooler days to come. At the back of the vegetable garden great sunflowers flaunted their gayety. Borders of rosemary and garden herbs—mint, thyme, sage, parsley, sweet basil and rows of peppers gave a variety of flavorings for kitchen use.

As a little child I reveled in the roses. My mother would take me out among them and often we would pull the petals from a great lapful and sprinkle them in the bureau drawers and among the clean linen. A more delightful perfume I have not known. It was about this time that Dr. Noisette, a Huguenot resident of Charleston, South Carolina, was propagating the Noisette, his exquisitely lovely tea roses, which he afterwards placed upon the market.

There were some enjoyable visits to the home of my maternal grandparents the Ellarbee family—just a few miles away. From the front piazza of this home one could look down two roads, the one leading to the river bridge, the other to the county courthouse, less than a mile distant. I remember in the front yard a large shrub with drooping purple flowers. I saw some of these old-fashioned flowers not long ago—the first I have seen in many years.

My grandfather Ellarbee was a stout, good-natured, middle-aged man, very fond of his pipe. I was fond of grandfather but did not like his pipe. All the men of that time were accomplished horseback riders. I remember a certain horse that this grandfather used to ride—a dark chestnut sorrel. I have forgotten other names less hard to recall, but I have never forgotten the name of that horse. How it came I do not know. The name was Rashe possibly it was spelled Reche.

My mother had several younger sisters and they always made a great ado over her children. The youngest sister was only five or six years older than myself and still played dolls. There was another little girl in the neighborhood who used to come with her parents at the same time. When this child was there we all played dolls, and with the dramatic instinct possessed by most children we would play "lady" in some of the cast off finery of the elder sisters in the family.

In the big "hall" (combination living room and dining room) a very large sideboard occupied several feet on one side of the room. Over it hung a picture that had for me a peculiar fascination. I do not know what became of this picture but I have never forgotten it. Years afterward Grandmother told me that its title was "The Drunkard's Career." I used to climb up in a chair and study the picture for long intervals. It was a series of scenes rather than one picture; the first represented a young man, handsome and dressed in evening clothes, taking a social glass; in the next he was a little tipsy; later on very drunk and engaged in a bar-room brawl; and so on down to the last which, tho the worst of all and somewhat gruesome in its features, held me, so that I can close my eyes after all these years and see it as then—a small covered wagon with a driver on the front seat driving a poor disreputable looking horse. No other creature was in sight save a half-starved small dog following the wagon. Grandmother put me off when I questioned—said the owner of the dog was dead and the dog was grieving for his master; that people ought not to drink liquor for it made them drunk, and drunkenness was very dreadful. Part of this explanation was lost on me at the time as Grandmother probably meant it should be. I had never seen anybody drunk and the idea of death was very vague. But it passes me to this day how even the most ardent temperance advocate could bear to have such a picture over the family sideboard—reminder and warning tho it might be. I loved the picture of the Madonna and Child at home. The Baby was so beautiful it gave me great delight to look at it.

I should like to speak further of this maternal grandmother Ellarbee. I was too young then to define my feeling toward her childish admiration rather than love, and while I never lost that admiration for Grandmother, it was not until years afterward, in my adult life, that I came to know and really appreciate the many fine attributes of her character. I think little children accept the members of their family as a matter of course and easily adapt themselves to those around them. In those very early days Grandmother was Grandmother, a personage of some importance whom everybody should look up to and honor.

When Grandmother gave me any special attention I was glad, but beyond an affectionate little greeting and goodbye on the occasion of my visits she never caressed me. She was uniformly kind but not demonstrative. There was no clinging to her with words of endearment, no exchange of homely little pet names, so common between most grandmothers and children. There was no appearance of coldness or hardness about Grandmother, she was a fine looking woman of dignified but agreeable appearance, and people yielded her ready deference. As I knew her later, she seemed a philosopher. A woman of strong mentality, her standards of word and action were high— womanly woman, but the caliber of her mind had masculine quality. It was handed down that she was very like her father, whose youngest child she was. He had been a gallant young officer in the American Revolution and had lived to a very advanced age.

Just a few years from the time of which I am speaking Grandfather Ellarbee died, leaving Grandmother with a family not all of adult age. With fine executive ability she assumed the added cares, ruled her household, trained her young sons and daughters for the higher duties of life, and dispensed the hospitality of her home. Much of the material prosperity which the family enjoyed was due to Grandmother's individual efforts. She was the wise woman described by King Solomon—"She looketh well to the ways of her household." A woman who could be depended upon in an emergency, the neighbors went to her for counsel and Grandmother went to them in their times of sickness and sorrow. Whatever of tenderness she possessed lay deep and found expression in deeds, not words, but she blessed the world in which she lived. I have studied Grandmother; she had wit, but little sense of humor. I never remember hearing her laugh a good shaky laugh; no one indulged in levity in her presence; and tho with her calm dignity she rarely offered a reproof, even the children got outside to "cut up."

The most remarkable and unusual thing about Grandmother was the attitude of her several sons-in-law toward her. Only one called her "Mother," but each and all loved her as if she had been mother in fact. That grandmother of mine was a wonderful woman, one of the most wonderful I have known. I am proud to have received my middle name from her thru my own mother—Elizabeth.

But to return to my own home. The chief source of revenue was livestock. In earlier times it had been rice and other grains. The rice was put into large casks, rolled down to the river by means of a wheel and axle arrangement, and there loaded on to barges and taken to the city where large rice mills turned out the finished product. The impress of the old "rolling roads" was left long after their use was discarded.

On the very large river plantations where the cultivation of rice was the one industry, they had their own mills for hulling and cleaning. Rice was a very important article of food. What was needed for home use on the smaller places was hulled and cleaned by hand.

This process was carried on in a deep wooden mortar with heavy wooden pestle. The pestle was sometimes operated after the manner of the old fashioned wellsweep. With this leverage the work of pounding the pestle was much easier. The product thus turned out was the same as the "brown rice" so much exploited at the present time. The winnowing was done by hand. A large round tray made of coarse heavy grass and very narrow binding strips of sturdy cane, was dexterously handled by the Negro beating the rice. Mounting a little platform and turning the tray about to catch the breeze, he soon had the chaff blown away.

The tray, known as a fanner, was used for many purposes. Negro hucksters in the city market used the fanner to pile up their truck. The Negro street venders would carry heavily loaded fanners of vegetables and fruit on their heads. The ability to poise loads on their heads was possessed by most Negroes of that time. It seemed a favorite way for them to carry burdens, as a basket or bundle of clothes, and even a full pail of water in perfect safety.

We had large numbers of cattle-more than needed to be cared for on the home place. I have been told there were three settled places on our land, each having a comfortable farmhouse and buildings with enough cleared land to provide for a family. These places, stocked with cattle, my father let to smaller farmers free of rent, only the farmer was to take care of the stock and use it nearly as his own. If his help was needed on the home place in marking and branding the cattle, he was to render this service, for which there was some sort of compensation. The poorer who lived under these conditions considered himself fortunate to secure this arrangement which, if he were industrious and careful, opened up the way of making a competence for himself and family. Moreover, they were treated as neighbors and friends, tho not equal in social standing—I wonder if this economic adjustment was a relic of the old feudal system?

Cattle gathering always took place in the spring of the year when there was a large number of new calves. Tho the winters were mild, the coming of spring was always pleasantly anticipated. Bluebirds were the earliest harbingers, then bob white, and after the whippoorwill was first heard in the night there was no further fear of cold that might blight the early fruit. Then the rounding up of the cattle began. Whippoorwills are associated in my mind with the cows and the sweet spring and summer time. "Whippoor-will" and "Jack married a widow," repeated with gay frequency, marked the evenings and early night of all the season.

It was a great privilege to go to the cowpens where the cows were milked in the open. The calves had been kept in a shady little pasture thru the day and were now brought to their mothers. Raising the calves was very important, so only a portion of the milk was taken from the mothers. The Negro children had to mind the calves while the milking was going on, as the calves would try to assert their rights to all the milk. This was all so interesting, also the naming of the cows—Brindle and Dun, Whitey, Sukey and Butterfly were regular stock names. The children would claim certain ones—those they thought prettiest.

After the calves had taken the share of milk allotted to them they were divided off, the calves turned out and the mothers kept in the cowpen until morning when, at a very early hour while the dew was still on the grass, the cows who had been lying down and ruminating all night would be milked again, turned out and driven to pasture or to the open woods to graze; the calves went back to their little pasture. This was the schedule for the summer months. A very few of the best milkers were kept up and fed to supply the family needs in winter.

The goats had a house of their own, off in an oak grove at some distance from the home. It was made of logs with great cracks between. It is well known that goats are not fond of water and the house was simply to afford them shelter in time of rain and storm. If only a light shower came up the goats would be seen running for their shelter.

Hogs were allowed to run at large until late summer and early fall, feeding on pine mass (the seed of the pine trees). They were then put into the fields to fatten on peanuts or chufas and potatoes, and later penned up and corn-fed for the market or the home table. When the weather became cold there was a busy time, "hog killing." The year's supply of meats—bacon, sides, hams, and sausage—was hung up in the end of the big smokehouse and cured to the degree of perfection. A plantation smokehouse is an interesting place to visit. Seeing such quantities of meat hanging from the poles it was a wonder how so much could be consumed in addition to the fresh meat, game and fish available thruout the year; but the Negroes had to be fed in addition to the family, and it took large quantities for the strong men working on the farm and with the timber.

The kitchen was some yards from the main dwelling. This was to lessen the danger of fire. Sometimes there was a covered platform between the two buildings but often this was dispensed with. Even now, an elderly Southern lady when in her kitchen may speak of the dining room as "the house."

The cooking was done on a large open fireplace with the aid of various pots and pans, as spiders, skillets, racks and broilers, long-handled waffle-irons, wafer-irons and toasters. There was plenty of wood of all kinds—oak, hickory and lightwood (this last for kindling or for torchlights). Meats and game were broiled before an open fire on oak or hickory coals with a pan to catch the juices, or were roasted in big iron ovens. Wild turkey roasted on a spit before the fire with frequent turnings and bastings, roast duck, and fried chicken, juicy and brown, were ordinary delicacies. All these good things took time and labor to prepare, but the main cook always had plenty of helpers.

In the basement of some very old homes of Southern cities there may be even now a walled-up mass of brick that is not solid masonry but was once a great oven; I have seen some that were no longer in use. They were heated with live coals from the kitchen fireplace, the coals then raked out and the food, meats or pastry, placed inside, the heavy iron door was closed and the food left to bake. This mode of baking was said to have given excellent results in the quality of the products, but it seems to have been a laborious method of preparation.

Maum Rhina was famous for lightbread as well as for the other good things she prepared. She made the yeast and set it aside to rise—in the sun in summer, or in a warm place on the kitchen hearth in winter. About the middle of the afternoon she would have the sponge ready to bake. In warm weather she would find a clean place in the back yard under the shade of a tree. The big iron oven, several inches deep, would be brought out with the dough in it, the lid carefully placed. There would be pine burs or corn cobs to start with. Taking her seat on a low stool, the old woman would light a thin blaze below and on the top of the oven, slowly and gradually warming it but not raising the temperature very much at first. When she found the sponge sufficiently risen, she would start baking with a slow, steady fire of twigs and chips. The entire process would take an hour or more. The bread was most delicious; served with sweet home-made butter there was nothing finer.

In the backyard there was a very large iron pot in which the food for the fourteen hound dogs my father kept had to be cooked, this in addition to some raw meat that was given them. The duty of feeding and caring for the dogs fell to a half-grown Negro boy in whom my father put much confidence. The dogs were not allowed to eat any food that was quite hot, lest it impair their power of scent. A dog's nose is always cold.

Wide, open fireplaces and wood fires were the rule. We used some lamps, and a new illuminating "fluid" was being introduced, but candles were our main dependence for lighting the home. Kerosene came later. Our best candles, for the brass and silver candle-sticks, were bought in the city; there the streets and many of the best homes were lighted by gas. Moulding the homemade candles, polishing the brass andirons, polishing the mahogany dining table, were duties assigned to one Negro. These with keeping wood for the hall and the bedrooms and having the hearth neat and well swept in the season of fires, were important duties, and usually well performed.

One of the most interesting and pleasurable experiences was when my father would take my mother and the children to the river to watch the rafting of the timber. The occasion was considered a great frolic. Huge pine logs were cut down and hauled to the river bluff, there sent down to the water and made ready to be taken to Savannah the city market. There were no motor trucks or tractors in those days. The hauling was done by oxen, the logs being lashed to big timber carriages. After the logs were launched and rafted, the men going on the trip would get their camping outfit ready. In addition to hampers of cooked food there had to be some facilities for cooking on the raft. Skillets and pots, notably a big coffee pot, were brought forth. The rafts were generally manned by white men, and sometimes the master would go along to see that things were rightly done. The great rafts, often there were several, were floated down into the larger Ogeechee River and on to the sea. Then the danger started. If the weather was fair the trip along the seacoast, and up the river to Savannah where the lumber was marketed, would be made without great event; but if a storm arose, as is quite likely on that part of the South Atlantic coast at certain seasons of the year, there might be loss of part of the fleet and the lives of the men imperiled. It was the usual purpose to avoid the season of storms but it could not always be done. Some years earlier the Ogeechee canal had been dug to shortened the distance between the Ogeechee River near home and the Savannah on which the market city was located; however the danger and adventure of the longer trip had its appeal to the men of that time and they did not entirely abandon it for the shorter and less hazardous route thru the canal. The trip by the seacoast and return would consume about a week, dependent upon the weather and the time spent in the city. The men always came back in teams that were sent to Savannah for them. I have heard many exciting tales told of storms encountered on the South Atlantic by lumbermen on the log rafts. There was much adventure and danger, but really very little loss of life.

The round of activities in farm life, always interesting, was more so, perhaps, when the features were varied and less dependence was placed upon outside help. True, there was sometimes a division of labor among neighbors that was mutually helpful. One man might be a better veterinarian than another; one might have a better equipped blacksmith and wheelwright shop; another a larger and better cotton gin; while still another might have a leaning toward medicine and have studied somewhat, so that if the regular family doctor who lived twenty miles or more away could not be reached whenever wanted (since there were no rural telephones and no automobiles), this neighbor could be relied upon to prescribe simple household remedies.

After preparing the land and planting the crops in Spring, came the marking and branding of cattle, shearing the sheep and marketing the lambs and the wool; driving hogs and cattle by slow stages to the city market. Butter was sent in large quantities, also lard and cured meats. There were hay cutting, corn gathering, cotton picking, ginning and baling. All these furnished a busy round of duties, yet where the business was systematized there was ample leisure for everybody to enjoy life. Mind you, I am speaking of the late slavery period; there came a time later, and before the invention and general use of so many labor-saving machines and appliances, that life on the farm was one strenuous round of hardships, particularly for the women.

In those older days people took pride in having an appearance of prosperity evidenced by a number of servants to do the work. Farm life when humanely conducted—and it generally was—made no greater hardship for the Negroes than now for strong brawny men.

The Negroes usually had their Saturday afternoons off from work. Many of them owned a dog (and strange to say the yellow cur was the favorite). They had coon and possum hunting, their banjo playing, and dancing in the quarters, which was generally permitted. Anent dancing, note certain very popular dances taken up by members of the smart set in these later modern days, that are known and recognized as having had their origin among the Southern Negroes. All in all, the lot of those Negroes was not the most miserable existence in the world. At least they had no care for the morrow and the needs of the wherewithal to live.

But freedom is sweet and the slave owners, by the emancipation of the slaves, have been relieved of a very large part of the "White Man's Burden,"—a burden that really enslaved the masters. LONG LIVE FREEDOM.

## 2

LIFE OVER THE RIVER—CANOOCHEE-OGEECEHEE

Not yet have I exhausted the list of things I remember about the "Old Place,"—the old river cove plantation and its beautiful idyllic life, but there are other things to record of a somewhat later time.

When my paternal grandfather died, a little while before my father's marriage, he left a will bequeathing the greater part of his then estate to my father, but the will was not legally recorded before his death (which occurred immediately after). The other children, of whom there were five—three sons, and one daughter older and the other my father's junior, and all married, came in for an equal share in the estate, altho they had each received a handsome portion when they had married and left home. My father would not contest, but agreed to an equal division with the others. When my father's mother passed away, about two years after her husband, there was another division. This all resulted in my father's receiving the old home place, but fewer slaves and other property. This was a valuable landed property, for which my father had a strong sentimental attachment, and he was satisfied.

The family removal which I have previously mentioned, took us over the Canoochee River only a few miles away, where my father entered what one of the neighbors spoke of as the mercantile business—a large general store that supplied goods of all kinds to a wide area many miles in extent. The farming operations were circumscribed; the timber interests were taken care of by one of my mother's brothers on the old place. The number of slaves was not large, and occupation was found for all of them.

The store and home were located on a broad highway that ran for miles, thru several counties, into the interior of the state and found one terminus in the city of Savannah, less than twenty-five miles away. The railroad station, now the Atlantic Coast Line, was some miles from our place, and portions of the back counties were not reached by the railroad at all. It was rich farming country, and where water transportation was not available the interchange of agricultural products and manufactured goods was by teams drawn by mules. Great loaded wagons, some of them en train, piled high with bales of cotton and every other conceivable farm product, went down to the city and brought back equally loaded wagons of merchandise of various sorts. Even country merchants adopted this means of transfer; it meant adding a few more miles to what was required to reach the railroad station and reloading to complete the route by rail, with the necessity of making schedule time, as against sixty, seventy, or more miles to market by the highway and no unloading before the city was reached, with the schedule arranged to meet personal convenience.

Often the loaded wagons traveled by night and rested by day when the weather made it desirable. One, two, or three nights might be spent on the road both going and coming, and this required a camping outfit for each team, as the men usually preferred to spend the night in the open to stopping in some home along the route. Friendly people who came to know the teamsters and exchanged gossip with them (newspapers were not so common then), often provided facilities for camping. Wells of cool water were often along the wayside to welcome travelers, men and animals alike.

The great highway which ran by our home was one of the important roads in the state. It led in an almost straight line inland from the coast for more than one hundred miles. Locally it was known as the "Hencart Road," from the great numbers of live poultry carried over it to the city market. They were ranged in tiers upon the wagons and had to be taken along in the cool of the day, fed and watered at proper intervals.

There were several good roads built by slave labor, and tho not so good as our present day hard-surfaced roads, many of them afforded easy, if slower, means of communication. One magnificent road led practically all the way from Savannah, across the ferry over the Great Ogeechee River, and on thru two counties along the seacoast. This was the old Darien Stage Road. Before the construction of the railroad, and even down to very recent times, when it was included in the system of state highways, the Darien Road was largely traveled and was a memorial to the people who planned and the slaves who built it—a large part with causeways and corduroy structures, thru the lowland swamps.

There were two ways by which we went to the city; the shorter by several miles was to follow the great highway and cross the Ogeechee River by ferry. Although the river was very wide at this point the ferry was considered safe. The other way was by the bridges, crossing first our own Canoochee River near home which was a tributary of the larger one, then a few miles further crossing by other bridges smaller tributaries, the Little Ogeechee and the larger river, above the ferry where the streams were not so wide (and where one did not get so nervous). More than one splendid bridge has been built over the great expanse of that big Ogeechee River since that time. A magnificent structure spans it now and there is much traffic.

After the death of my maternal grandfather Ellarbee, grand-mother moved to Savannah where two married daughters were living. She was a woman with vision far beyond the day in which she lived. Her fine executive ability and splendid talent for business won for her honorable and substantial recognition. She was a pioneer business woman. Clan loyalty and family devotion were strong traits with us, and my parents made frequent visits to see "Mother and the girls." The trip could be made in a few hours and we had a strong family horse who was an excellent traveler. With this horse in a light rockaway (surrey) and a trusty servant to drive, my mother would often start off in the early morning with the three children, leaving father with Maum Delia and Flora to look after his needs (and Maum Rhina to boss them). We would probably come back the second afternoon. When mother took us children and was accompanied by only a servant for protection, we always went the longer way,—the bridge road. Mother could shoot, and could hit a mark pretty accurately. She may have carried a pistol for greater safety when we reached the section where the rice fields lay not far from the road. I believe she did have a pistol, but it was not told to the children and we were quite happy and gay, and no trouble of any kind ever befell us.

The road from Savannah to where two roads forked (the one from the ferry and the one from the bridge) was laid with heavy plank, a distance of twelve miles, and it was a very popular drive. "Two-forty on the plank road" was the slogan for speed. Tho it has been greatly excelled since them, it was the best record made by any trotting horse at the time. Many stylish equipages and gay cavalcades were to be seen on the plank road every afternoon. A little before we met the fashionable crowd, my mother would have us stop and furbish up our toilets, then we could enter the city in proper trim to the clatter of our horse's hoofs—always a pleasant sound to me. A few feet from the roadside at one place was a spring of pure bubbling water that no one had attempted to commercialize. It has been properly curbed by the owner and was kept in sanitary condition for the use of the traveling public. Truly that man was a public benefactor.

When my father went with us to town we generally stayed several days. Sometimes the visit would combine business with pleasure. In the evening the children would be left with a careful servant in Grandmother's home and the others would go to the show. I used to wonder, curiously, what was meant by "the show" and once asked to go, but my mother said children ought not to sit up so late and I must go to bed as usual. Once, however I remember father insisted on taking us to see the bears. They were in a tent. There was a dancing bear and a great big bear in a cage. Something caused the big bear to growl, which frightened me very much. A big little boy tried to allay my fears by talking to me in a very superior way about his lack of fear of the bear I was then a timid little soul, and my terror of the bear, an annoyance at the strange boy talking to me, caused me such real distress that my father took us all away, much to the disappointment of the other children who wished to stay longer.

My father was a young man as I remember him then. He was a little more than twenty-five years of age when I was born. It seems a pleasant thing for children to know their parents while the parents are still in their youth. My father was a man the women loved and trusted. He had a tender reverence for womanhood and a way that drew little children to him. I recall him in the dress of a gentleman of that period, which for street wear and daytime public functions was rigid in its formality—the inevitable high silk hat, boots polished like a mirror (every dressing room closet had its boot-jack), frock coat and pantaloons of black broadcloth, flowered satin waistcoat, linen of immaculate whiteness laid in plaits, and above this a high collar and black satin stock. Over all this elegance was worn a long military

cloak of heavy broadcloth, lined with handsome woolen material of
Scotch plaid, with high choker collar for winter wear. En passant,
some years later during the War Between the States, my mother had
a tailor cut this same handsome cloak into two little suits—jacket
and trousers—for my small brothers, else there would have been no
Sunday suits for their little bodies. About this period the black satin
stock was being discarded for a broad cravat and high linen collar, the
latter quite stiff and with corners pointed. The clerical collar, popular
for so many years after, was not so high, but the points came well up
against the face. For dignified occasions young men carried a light
cane. If the man were old, it was usually a heavy gold-headed cane,
often the gift of admiring friends.

The Canoochee River bridge was very near our new home but
the river was not in sight because of the trees and a swamp beyond.
The river boatmen often carried a long bugle—I have seen some that
were fully five feet in length. Our house was large and much in the late
style of the time; often as we sat on the piazza on warm, moonlight
nights we could hear the merry tunes played on the bugle as boats
passed the bridge—less than a mile away. When there was no moon
the firestands were lighted, one each side of the front gate. These
were table-shaped platforms covered with a heavy layer of sand or
clay and on this lightwood fires were built, to lighten the darkness
and to drive away the mosquitoes that came in season. In that section
we were not troubled with the minute sandflies that make the smudge
a nightly necessity along the coast in warm weather.

I have said that our house was in a sort of modern style, but I
do not believe my mother ever really enjoyed it, there being a showy
pretense about it that did not make for comfort. It was not of our
planning. Father bought it ready built from a family who had spent
more money on it than they could afford and were glad to get back
what they had put into it. The place was very near the store and stock
of goods purchased at the time, and it suited us to live there. However,
thru two successive sales and purchases the place was owned by some
member of my mother's family for more than fifty years.

Twice a year there was much bustle in our immediate
community—during court week. The Circuit, or Superior Court,
as it was known, held regular sessions in the Spring and Fall. My
father had many friends among the legal fraternity, many of the older

members of the bar having been friends of his father. In earlier days, in the old plantation home, open house was kept for the judge and certain others, many of them distinguished men of the state. It was considered a privilege to be entertained in my grandparents' home, with its comforts and open hospitality. Other homes, very comfortable in their way, took care of many guests. The Southerners of that legal coterie were all more or less gifted with the talent of oratory and their coming to our quiet country community for a sojourn of a week or more was always welcomed.

A sort of coincidence occurs just here. The office of Probate Judge, as it is called in some states, but in this state the Ordinary, was held for many decades by some member of my father's or my mother's family. Incumbents for long terms were my father's oldest brother, mother's oldest brother and her nephew; and for shorter periods the office was held by cousins of my father.

The old plantation church, Macedonia, was in a large grove just off the river bridge and near our home. Here people from miles around came to worship. A space in the back of the church was railed off for the Negroes who accompanied their masters. Some of these Negroes were regular communicants in the church, and when the sacrament was administered they sat a little in the rear of the white people, and the elements were passed to them in reverent sincerity.

The people of the community ranked as genteel country folk, mostly farmers or planters. There were two or three very wealthy planters from the lower part of the county, my Aunt Edith's family and one overseer, who had their Negro coachmen, but most of the gentlemen drove their own teams. One very popular style of family carriage was the rockaway or surrey. The courting couples generally came to church in buggies; the gentleman driving and landing in the grove very near the church where everyone could see, with a great flourish would assist the lady to alight from the vehicle. This gesture was not lost upon any of the onlookers, each of whom had an individual way of approving or disapproving. The girl, with the demure manner of the time, being the cynosure of all eyes, outwardly somewhat embarrassed but secretly elated over the little ripple of interest they had caused, walked gracefully by the gentleman's side and they both entered the church.

At "quarterly meeting," or at other times, there would be both morning and afternoon service. On such occasions dinner would be spread on long tables under the great oak trees. Then, extra Negro servants would be brought to assist in laying the dinner and caring for the lunch baskets. If ever a table groaned, those rough wooden tables with snowy linen cloth had reason to do so. Every conceivable kind of good thing to eat was there in abundance. There was much cheerful rivalry on the part of the housewives and their Negro cooks as to the quality and quantity of viands offered. Culinary skill was carried to the highest and most artistic degree. Anybody, particularly strangers from beyond the neighborhood, would be made welcome and urged to eat. In pleasant weather little children were kept by their nurses in the carriages out of doors during services. Choir practice was held some time before morning worship, but most of the young people who led the music had been to the singing school that was always held one evening during the week. Happy, Happy, Days!

I remember a country church a few miles on the other side of the river, which we sometimes visited. A family who lived near that church always entertained as many of their neighbors as they could. After services at the church were concluded invitations were given out—and were expected to be accepted. If you declined the invitation you felt guilty of rudeness. This family, tho' not rich had a fair share of this world's goods, and seemed to get much pleasure out of their lavish hospitality. There were several children in the family and while the father and mother were in many ways exemplary people they were said to be most lax in parental discipline. The larger boys in company with Negro youth of about their own age were permitted to roam the fields and woods, hunting, fishing and idling away the time when they should have been in school. The girls at home governed themselves. While none of these children seemed at all vicious, they were just no good, according to general verdict, and the worst children in the county. As they grew up none of them chose a life of evil, or ever came under the condemnation of the law; two or three turned out fairly well, but the others were just ne'er-do-well. The little schooling that any of them ever received was from a private teacher or governess; these came periodically, stayed awhile, went, and never returned.

One Sunday my father and mother stayed to dinner at this home, having been greatly urged. The house was large, with a wide verandah on three sides. The ladies among the visitors were invited into a large bedroom where they left their bonnets, wraps and parasols on the great feather bed. After dinner, when their elders were engaged in conversation on the front verandah, some of the kids took a notion to have a good time dressing themselves up in the things left by the visiting ladies in the bedroom. I did not feel at home with those little girls and stood outside looking in at them. What was my consternation to see one of the smaller girls array herself in my mother's lovely new bonnet and silk mantilla, hoist my mother's dainty parasol above her head and prance around the room. I just couldn't stand it. I loved to "play lady" as much as a natural-minded child, but always had permission to dress up in discarded or, at least, last year's finery. In some way I managed to communicate with my mother who rescued her things in time to prevent any great damage, and to intimate to my father, in a tactful way, that it was time to go home. I do not remember that we ever stayed to dinner with those good people again, tho my father sometimes invited the old gentleman to dinner when he came to the store to trade.

One of my father's brothers (his senior by fifteen years) was Uncle John, a dapper little gentleman with a dignity of bearing that attested his self-esteem, tho the merry twinkle in his eye betokened a sense of humor. Uncle John's cheeks were like two red apples. He reminded one of the less rugged type of Scotchman, and seeing him you might wonder sometimes how he would look in plaid and kilts. It was said that he had played the violin with excellence in his youth and had been very fond of dancing, but, as I remember Uncle John first, he was well along in a fifty-year old official membership in a church that prohibited dancing altogether and did not greatly approve of "fiddling" by the leading members. Uncle John's musical performances, tho much appreciated by his family and friends, may have been only fiddling. He had married his wife when she was just a girl in her early teens. Aunt Sophia was the same age as my father and fifteen years her husband's junior. The match had been arranged by their respective families and gave satisfaction all around. A later marriage occurred between the two families when my father's younger sister became the wife of a son of the other family, Aunt Sophia's brother.

In spite of the disparity in their ages, I have never known a married couple who were more devoted to each other. For fifty years they walked hand in hand thru life, thru its joys and sorrows, thru peace and war time, prosperity and adversity, unswerving in their faith in each other and faith in God, until at a ripe old age, Uncle John passed into the Great Beyond. The little wife did not long survive. Their graves are side by side in the family graveyard, near the ruins of the old church they loved so well. They trained their sons and daughters for lives of usefulness, and so blessed the world in which they lived.

As children we liked to visit our cousins, who came to see us in return. At Uncle John's there was much freedom of speech, and much humor but always kindliness and courtesy. I do not remember ever hearing an unkind speech from any one of them, though once the oldest son, Jimmy, did receive a severe reprimand for his tactlessness; but the boy enjoyed the "joke" as he called it. The father sometime before that had brought a horse from a gentleman in an adjoining county, which had become the horse that the boys and girls were privileged to drive about the neighborhood, attached to an old buggy. An unusual visit over night from the former owner of the horse was being concluded by a pleasant conversation on the front piazza next morning, when Jimmy's voice was heard giving orders to one of the Negro boys to "harness old Bradley and bring him round to the front." *Bradley* was the gentleman's name and the family had by common consent decided to call the horse by the name of his former owner, and had prefixed the term *old*.

Have you ever noticed the use of the word old by Southern people in their everyday speech? It is a very flexible term with many meanings. It may be used for endearment, hatred, contempt, or casually as an expletive. "That little old baby" or "the little old thing" are expressions of love and tenderness, while "that old thing" may be the most contemptuous way to speak of anything, animate or inanimate. There is another peculiarity of speech. A Southern gentleman my invite you to "my house" meaning his home. In a certain section of two adjoining states we hear "right much." Familiar little touches of homely phrase add to rather than detract from the charm of social life.

At that time manners were more formal, even among the younger set. A gentleman never addressed a young girl without the prefix "Miss" unless he had always known her. In like manner even a mature woman would not call a young man of short acquaintance by his first name. That was a privilege accorded to his mother's friends or to near relatives. Very young men, or younger sons, might be known as "Mr. John" or "Mr. Charley." It was the custom among the higher classes for a married woman to address her husband as "Mister"—even when speaking to him directly or in private. There was no touch of servility in this; it was correct form. Engagements of marriage were not always announced as soon as made, as they are now. A gentleman might be "waiting upon" or "addressing" a lady—in school-girl parlance—"paying his distresses" to her. A girl might indicate to a gentleman caller in some subtle way that his next call would be agreeable to her but it was from her mother that the direct invitation came, if it came at all. Some of those old conventions and artificial restraints have well been set aside. Manners may not be so fine now but they are more natural, with less pretense and make-believe.

# 3

## LIFE AMONG THE NEGROES

The largest aggregations of slaves, perhaps, were found on the cotton plantations of the Sea Islands and the rice plantations of the coast. These Negroes were less intelligent than the Negroes who came in contact with the white people. In South Carolina the rice field Negroes were known as "Gullah" Negroes, while those in the rice fields of Georgia were largely "Geechee," so called from the Ogeechee River that drains so much of that section and afforded water for the cultivation of the miles of low-lying rice fields. Just below the Ogeechee were two other river districts, the Altamaha (or Darien) and the Satilla (or Brunswick). These rice fields had been under cultivation a great many years, but owing to intelligent management and the use of the water system, had not lost their fertility. Each plantation had its overseer (in Geechee parlance "Der Obershur"), assisted by some younger man who was learning the business of rice culture, and one of the mature and more experienced plantation Negroes. This Negro held the place of leader among his own people and was a man of large influence with the blacks. They never questioned his authority—sometimes wielded with a heavy hand. Daddy or Uncle Primus was a most useful man on the plantation and rarely betrayed the confidence placed in him by his white superiors. Indeed, the feeling between them was one of kindliness and friendship, tho the black man never "forgot his place."

On the larger plantations a regular physician was employed to administer to them, and a trained clergyman to preach to them at regular intervals. The doctor had to be a man of ability. The preacher might not be among the most talented in his profession, but he needed to be specially fitted for his work—a man of tact and piety, possessed of the missionary spirit and with intelligent sympathy for

his charges, patient, kind, and worthy of trust and confidence. There
was no pretense of attempting to educate the slaves except morally
and in the basic principles of health and decent living. Their own
preachers exhorted them. Tho the Negro preachers were themselves
ignorant, their influence in the main was good.

The rice field Negroes more than any others had their shouting
parties that were very often wild orgies and must have been a relic
of their former state of savagery. The shoutings could be heard a
long way off. An account of their belief in hoodoos, witch doctors,
conjuring, "sperrits" and other superstitions, would make a long
chapter. All ancient peoples had their superstitious beliefs, founded
upon ignorance of natural laws, but since science has done so much
to dispel that ignorance there are few intelligent individuals of the
present day who would willingly admit that their minds harbor
even the milder forms of superstition. Yet, so firm a hold upon the
youthful mind have the things we learned in childhood, few of those
brought up with Negro nurses are really free of every vestige of
superstition.

My mother was a very careful mother and vigilant in her efforts
to guard her children from all evil influences. "Jack the Giant
Killer" and tales of like character were taboo in our home, but we
heard about "Raw Head and Bloody Bones" from Uncle Charles, a
favorite old Negro man. From Jane, a young house girl, I heard such
wonderful stories of haunted houses, in which our own home figured
extensively, that I became afraid to go from one room to another in
the dark, or upstairs by myself in the daytime. My mother and father
were some time in discovering the cause of my extreme nervousness,
but when they did there was a reckoning with Jane which she was
likely to remember.

Where the Negroes were fewer in number they had exhortations
from the master or an occasional white minister, and those who
wished were permitted to join the church of the white people.
These were mostly family servants. In the city one of the long upper
galleries of the church would be reserved exclusively for its Negro
members. In addition there were several large city churches for the
Negroes only, and their membership ran into the hundreds. Some
of these old churches are standing today, monuments of the past,
and still affording places of worship, for the free colored people.

Some now have a church organ and trained choir in addition to the congregational singing, but the old-time singing was very wonderful in its way.

One picturesque feature of those far-away days has gone forever, the old turbaned Negress is seen no more. Then the custom was to have the Negro women wear (instead of the caps house servants wear now) a bandanna handkerchief wound neatly about the head—a "henkercher." On Sunday the younger women wore hats and dress bonnets, often from the mistress's cast off finery, but some of the oldest women—and who knows, how old many of them were—wore a high white turban.

This was made of fine white cambric with dainty border of fine colored stripes and a yard or more square. Beautifully laundered, it was wound with marvelous skill about the head into a structure a foot or more high, with not an unwanted wrinkle in its folds. To accompany the turban as part of the ensemble, was worn an apron of equally fine white cambric that came to the hem of the long skirt, covering the entire front of the dress; this too had been beautifully laundered. With the big white bows tied in the back, the woman thus attired was ready for any occasion. I have seen women dressed like this old enough to walk with a stick.

The old turbaned woman was an aristocrat among the Negroes. She was usually the superannuated appendage of some wealthy family whom she had served as nurse for two generations, or more, perhaps, and for that was entitled to much distinction in the family. The older members treated her with great kindness and respect, and the children accorded her a feeling of affection but little short of that they bestowed upon the oldest members of their own family.

The dress of this old woman ("Mauma" on the coast, "Mammy" farther up the country), was conspicuous, and worn ordinarily betokened her rank. She wore always earrings, very large hoops of gold, and these against her black face gave her a barbaric air. But the most wonderful part of her attire was the turban, which for Sundays and state occasions may have had just an added touch of dignity in height. As a child, when we were living in the city, I used to look across the large church to the gallery above, where sat one old turbaned mauma with dignified bearing. This old woman continued to occupy the same seat along with other Negroes even after they were freed, and probably until they died, as one by one they were seen no more.

The Negroes in the country other than the ricefield Negroes had their shouting parties, public baptizings and "distracted" meetings, at which their own preachers officiated with all the dignity and reverence they could command. They sang with clear musical voices beautiful spirituals—beautiful in melody if crude in literary form, and somewhat startling in phraseology if closely analyzed. The white people were always invited to the baptizings at the creek or by the riverside. The women candidates were dressed in white, the kind-hearted mistress furnished the costumes. If one of the house servants were to be baptized, the whole family including the children, were invited to witness the rites—an event looked forward to with much interest. These scenes by the water side were solemn and beautiful in character and with the singing left a distinct impression upon all present. Negroes are a very religious people and enjoy their religion.

The most weirdly solemn ceremony connected with the Negro life was the funeral. Burial took place at night by torchlight. This time was selected to permit Negroes from adjoining places in the neighborhood to attend, and seemed to be preferred for other reasons. They are a peculiar people and do not easily reveal themselves to the white race, study them as we may—an emotional people outwardly but often with deep hidden motives. They show a self-respecting shyness to intruders. When left to themselves they wanted their cabins in some secluded place, down in the hollow or amid the trees, with only a path to their abode. Yet when the time came for parades and pageants where they could show off they were ready enough.

Negroes are natural musicians. No higher or more coveted honor could come to one of them than to wield the baton for a drum corps or as leader of a band. Most of the dance music for the young white people in the South was furnished by Negro musicians. The performance may not have come up to critical standards but it served the purpose.

Communication between the blacks of neighboring plantations was by passport ("ticket"). In the city a Negro was not allowed on the streets after nightfall without a ticket, unless accompanying some white individual. I fancy the police were not very particular as to the authenticity of the signature, since children of the family were sometimes cajoled by a favorite servant into writing passports without due authority from the parents. But as the name and address of the owner, and the Negro as well, appeared on the passport there was not likely to be any trouble if the Negro behaved.

Negro men going "courtin" on another plantation had to get permission from the respective owners before they could take a wife. (This restriction was no greater than was placed upon the gentlemen of a somewhat earlier time, when the first advance toward courting a girl was to get permission from the father to address his daughter with a view to matrimony—a rather cold blooded formality in the light of the present day. That sort of thing might have been all right in arranging a marriage of policy and for reasons of state, where the girl was willing to be sacrificed on the altar of her country, but in Free America, NEVER).

The word "nigger" was not acceptable in polite speech, tho it was a term much in use among the Negroes themselves. At the present time the word is defended upon the ground of analogy and pronunciation. Furthermore, the Negroes were not spoken of as slaves except in political arguments, and if a gentleman said "my Negroes" there was no more arrogance intended than when he spoke of his home and family.

Names given the Negroes were a conglomerate lot, often being left to the wit or ingenuity of the white people unless some Negro parent particularly desired to bestow upon his offspring a certain name. Surnames not being specifically needed were left to the Negroes themselves. Sometimes the family name of the owner was adopted as their "entitle" but not always. Johnson, Jackson, and Williams were common surnames among them. As to the others, history, the classics and Holy Writ were their sources. In the same quarters might be found George Washington, "Gin'l Jackson," Lord Cornwallis, Napoleon Bonaparte (usually reduced to Bony Parts), Scipio (Africanus) Hannibal, Titus, Julius Caesar, Cato, Cupid, King Solomon, Simon Peter, and some celebrities of the day. The Bible names did not include the ugly Hebrew names that some of our early Americans in a mistaken religious zeal saddled upon their children. While there were numerous Jerrys and Zachs, the "Iahs" were left out. I am not sure that I ever heard of a Negro named Obadiah or Jeremiah.

The women's names were as fanciful as those of the men, and often very pretty. Juno, Minerva, Daphne, Venus, Phyllis, Chloe, the queens—Cleopatra, Esther, Charlotte, Victoria—then Flora, Violet, the stately Diana, and other beautiful feminine names. Sambo and Dinah were not typical names of the Southern slave Negroes. There were many Sams, and Dinah was nearly always Diana. Many lovely names were by common consent reserved for the Negroes. I do not remember anyone but a Negro being named Chloe; in like manner, John or Charles might be found in the quarters, but never the diminutive pet names Johnny or Charley.

Much credit is due to the slave of that time that they were so docile and easily managed, accepting the rule of the mistress for that of the master. Scarcely has such loyalty on the part of slaves been recorded of any other people. There was no thought of their disloyalty. This is in itself sufficient to establish the beneficent character of the Southern slavery. The attitude of loyalty was pronounced where the Negroes came into association with the white people. The more intelligent of their race seemed to consider themselves in some way allied to the white family. On the very large plantations the slaves were of a lower order of intellect and were kept in subjection by the overseer and his Negro assistant. Those Negroes rarely ever had a sight of their masters, and there was but little change in their condition wrought by the war until they were finally freed.

# 4

## LIFE AT TAYLORS CREEK

In the South there was general opposition to public schools. Intelligent, thoughtful parents were not so sure of the advantages to be derived from the general mixing of all the children of all classes and conditions of people. It was an experiment with caution. The Doctrine of States Rights was unswervingly and rigidly adhered to; the right of personal and individual freedom equally so. The education of their children was a private family affair, a matter in which no one, not even the state had the right to interpose. In a private school paid for from their own pockets they had a voice in determining what they were to get, they could and did dictate terms. This individual right would be relinquished in sending their children to a public school, where the curriculum and even the discipline was ordered by some other than the parent in most cases. There was no reputable public school in the nearby city.

In the populous communities there were very fine schools paid for directly by the patrons. In the thinly settled country districts well-to-do families employed a private teacher. Sometimes two or three families combined and established a neighborhood school. After this the boys and girls would frequently be sent away to preparatory school and college, or to boarding school. Not always, however, for means of communication and travel were so much slower then than now that parents were loath to send children very far from home. This did not mean that the young people grew up an uncultured lot. There was a standard of good manners and polite speech which came to them by inheritance. There were books in those days, some magazines and newspapers. It may be that more worthwhile books were read then than at a later period. There was more leisure for reading. Some narrow-minded individuals then objected to any fiction that passed

under the name of novels, but which dignified under some other
name they found very palatable. Much of the fiction of that day was
of the extreme romantic school. It was diverting, not really harmful
and could well be taken as sweets after the more serious stuff. It
satisfied the craving of youthful minds and beguiled many dull hours
for older readers.

About a mile above our home a primitive little schoolhouse had
been built to accommodate the boys and girls from two or three
families. The teacher, a large, blonde, elderly lady would frequently
spend the week-end in our home. My father and mother had taken
into their home an orphan boy to raise. Ferdinand was not an adopted
son, but a member of the family and treated with all kindness. I was
nearly old enough to go to school, and begged to be allowed to attend.
So the plan was that Ferdinand should ride to school on a slow and
perfectly safe old horse and that I should ride behind him on a pillow
or cushion. I liked that but held firmly to the boy's coat from the
back. Those were my first riding lessons. My brothers were taught, or
rather learned, to ride from the time they could sit on a horse. The art
of horsemanship was theirs by tradition and inheritance, perhaps.

My mother began to be seriously troubled about the education
of her children. In our immediate and not thickly settled community
there had never been any educational facilities. The only thing to do
was to sell out all our present possessions except the "Old Place,"
which my father loved next to wife and children, and move.

The thing was accomplished and we found ourselves in a new
community, Taylors Creek, among some acquaintances and a few
friends we had known before, where the educational facilities were
very fine. My father's business was of the same kind, but more
extended into a large department store. There was a fine well-to-do
patronage in the immediate locality, people of discriminating taste
and varied requirements. My father was in himself well fitted to
respond to the needs of this trade in the selection of his goods and
the methods of conducting the business. In addition to the home
trade, there was a large patronage from the rich farming section that
lay miles in extent in the more remote districts. Father bought their
cotton and wool and other farm products. In exchange he sold them
large supplies of manufactured goods. Frequently families came to
do their trading. The several young men, clerks and salesman in the

store, looked forward with pleasure to these visits of the farmers'
daughters.

Our house had a beautiful setting nearby, an immense oak tree
in front with fruit trees at the rear and sides. The house had been
remodeled and comfortably furnished under my mother's direction
and was large enough for the family and the greater social needs.

The Taylors Creek citizens were very proud of themselves, of
their lineage, gentility and refinement. Standards of human behavior
were very high indeed. There were many titles of distinction, some
genuine, some honorary or brevet. From the start of two or three
families they had married and intermarried until nearly everybody
was kin, and this kinship was acknowledged to the nth degree.

The very large and flourishing school was known as The
Academy. The curriculum was there and the teaching of a high order.
The school was presided over by a local clergyman, a man of scholarly
attainments and exalted character, a vital force in the neighborhood.
We had been living in the community only about a year when this
good man passed away.

The position as head of the school was then very unwisely put in
charge of a young man just out of college, a relative of some of the
most influential families. This young man was very vain and arrogant
and in no way suited to wear the mantle of his predecessor. However,
he ranked as a gentleman, and many who were not pleased with his
appointment accepted him as best they could for the unexpired term.
He did not succeed himself to office.

I have spoken of the standards of conduct as approved by
the Taylors Creek people. There were many artificialities and some
foolish conventions. Many of the restrictions fell rather heavily upon
the children. Boys were taught to remember that their grandfather
had been a gentleman. What that uncertain term meant each boy was
left to determine for himself. Little girls, poor things, were governed
by the standard of what was ladylike. This was ding-donged into their
ears day by day. No wonder that many of them, myself included,
became frightful little snobs.

One day at school two small girls had a falling out. One of
them emboldened by the fact of her kinship to the principal went
to him with tales against the other girl. Susie Birney declared that
Alice Winston had told Susie Birney that she, the said Susie Birney,

had repeated something that was not true, in fact that the said Susie Birney, in plain English had falsified—Alice Winston had used the shorter word—The gentleman principal, Mr. Patterson, was deeply and properly shocked, and announced to the whole school his grief and disappointment that a certain pupil had been charged with having used some very bad language, and he would look into the matter. That he might not act unduly or unwisely, he would make an investigation the next afternoon.

My mother never encouraged tattling and tale-bearing in her children, but everything that concerned them was of prime importance to her. I went to my mother with everything and it was due to her wise guidance after these confidences that my school life was made smooth and pleasant. Mistakes which I might otherwise have made did not occur.

The next night I announced with much excitement at home that Mr. Patterson was going to make a "vestigation" at school the next afternoon and if anybody had used bad language they would be punished.

I was given the proper counsel as to how to behave in this dreadful crisis. My fears were allayed as to the impending doom that was to fall upon the school, but a little child always dreads the unknown, and discord among elders is fraught with uneasiness. The next morning the little children were very quiet but watchful. Up to noon nothing unusual had happened. Many of the pupils who lived near the school always went home for lunch, but a greater number stayed. That day nearly everybody stayed. Just as the lunches had been disposed of, Sarah, the eldest Birney girl, assembled the Birney children, silently and swiftly, like a hen with a flock of chickens, headed the line and they all followed. I can see them now in my mind, Sarah, Martha, Susie, George P., and Lula, a little thin-legged girl, the youngest of the family. With books and lunch baskets, looking neither to right nor left, they took their course by a path thru the woods in the rear of the academy. This was the nearest way to the creek; their home was on the hill just beyond the bridge. I would like to speak of the Birneys, one of the best and most respected of the county families. They were substantial farmers. They had a large country home and were noted for their hospitality. The creek furnished power for their saw and grist mill; the millpond was a fine place to fish and many merry picnic parties were held there. Everybody loved "Uncle and Aunt Birney."

But to return to my story: The looked-for judicial trial did not come off. When I reached home that afternoon, I announced to my parents that "Mr. Patterson didn't have any 'vestigation,' because Susie went home." It transpired that Mrs. Birney had sent a note to the principal with the firm request that her children be dismissed at noon. The presence of Mrs. Birney's two big sons, members respectively of the junior and senior classes, might have had something to do with the ease with which the case was not pressed on the school calendar.

The next day affairs moved smoothly, but there was a tension in the air that did not wear off until the end of the week. Susie Birney was there as usual, but the other children by common consent seemed to withdraw from her. Whether Susie Birney had been guilty of falsehood as charged by Alice Winston, did not seem to matter so much as that Susie had committed the one offense that the entire juvenile world holds as unpardonable—she had carried tales to the teacher against a fellow pupil. Then, when trouble arose over her tale-bearing Susie went home.

I learned from this incident of my very early school life a lesson which stood me in good stead for many years. It was not the only time I have known individuals to stir up strife, and when about to be called to account, *Susie went home.*

Social life in Taylors Creek Community was pleasant if not exciting. The academy was made the social center. They had no formal baseball, and football as these games were unknown; but the students played catball, shinny, field hockey, hare and hounds, and leap frog. A boy with any agility at all could "skin the cat" on the horizontal bar. The children played their ring games, drop the handkerchief, prisoner's base.

At their juvenile parties they played forfeits with a few kissing games. There was one parlor game very popular. Thru its medium some interesting revelations were advanced. The young men retired usually to the front gallery, while the girls remained in the parlor. The young fellow who acted as master of ceremonies, after a brief whispered consultation with each of the girls, would go to the young men on the outside and announce to each of them in turn that he had been chosen as a mark of favor by one of the girls. The young man would thereupon enter and present himself before the young lady he thought had singled him out. If he guessed the right girl he was happy, but if he made a mistake everyone would know it and he would be "clapped out." Imagine the elation or the chagrin of the young men participants under the varying circumstances of this game. Perhaps they though with the Immortal Bard that:

> "He either fears his fate too much,
> Or his deserts are small,
> Who will not put it to the touch
> To win or lose it all."

Dancing was not looked upon with favor by their elders, but if they could find a parlor large enough or a hall, the young people on festive occasions would dance what some sophisticated ones called "Twistification," a form of the "Old Virginia Reel." In communities where there was no ban against dancing the beautiful square dances, the Cotillion and the graceful Lancers were introduced whenever available. There were plenty of stringed instruments and the music was generally good. Where there was no regular orchestra there would be found Negroes who furnished an excellent grade of dance music, for which the gentlemen paid them well.

Mock tournaments were a popular form of amusement with the young men, nearly all of whom were fine riders and liked to display their horsemanship and prowess. The successful knight was permitted to crown his lady—love queen of the festival. These tourneys, suggestive of the time "when knighthood was in flower" were sufficiently interesting to draw large crowds of fine people from adjoining counties.

The May Festival was a most elaborate affair. A large stage was erected under some of the giant oak trees on the campus. This was made a bower of beauty for the king and queen. The pageant included the usual array of maids of honor, garland bearers, flower girls and pages. Many gay house parties were held on these occasions, and much love making went on among the young people, and pleasantly smiled upon by their elders.

Across the creek, about a mile from our home was the Methodist campground. A large number of cottages, called "tents," some of them of a substantial character, other of a rude, transient sort had been built around a very large tabernacle. There were many good Methodist in our community and once a year, in the early fall, they held religious meetings at this place for a week. Some of the best pulpit orators and best singers in the denomination came from over the state to this noted campground. It was a magnificent exercise of hospitality on the part of the good people who built those cottages and welcomed any and all who would come and accept. No suggestion of payment for any accommodations received was permitted, but all were made welcome to the limit. True, there was much crowding, but there was an abundance of good food and much friendliness and good cheer. Everybody wore their best bib and tucker, and there was plenty of servants. I do not know of anything more conducive to good fellowship among the people of not only the same religious body, but with others as well, as was this splendid hospitality of the people of Taylors Creek, known all over the state. Several families who lived in the immediate neighborhood entertained at home. Carriage loads of visitors came and went to the services which were held morning, afternoon and night. Was there any shouting? Yes, in that day there were many sincere individuals who believed in shouting as a part of religious worship. You could shout if you felt like it. Some dear good women usually very meek and retiring were among the "happiest" of the shouters.[1]

---

1. The following news item from the Florida *Times-Union,* Oct. 26, 1930, shows that the camp meeting still flourishes at Taylors Creek:

LUDOWICI, Ga., Oct. 24-The Liberty County Methodist camp meeting which opened on October 17 came to a successful close Wednesday at Taylors Creek this being the one hundred and seventeenth annual session. The attendance was one of the largest assembled at the camp group in years and a larger number than customary made use of the 17 tents on the grounds.

Taylors Creek Church and camp meeting coming under the direction of the Waycross District, the Rev. James R. Webb, Presiding elder of the district had charge of the services, which were conducted by the visiting pastors, including: The Rev. W. A. Kelly, pastor Trinity Church, Waycross; the Rev. N, M. Lovein, general evangelist, Macon; and the local pastor, the Rev. J. D. McCord, Hinesville. Upon invitation, the Rev. J. F. Merrin, pastor of Flemington Presbyterian Church conducted the Sunday afternoon service.

W. J. Eitelgeorge of Canton, Ohio, choir director, conducted the song services.

A feature of the annual session was the annual meeting of the Martin clan, a social organization of Martins, the gathering being presided over by Emory S. Martin of Crescent City, Fla., who is national president of the organization. Interesting history of the Martins in this country and In Scotland were given by the speakers. At the election of officers those now in office were re-elected for the ensuing year.

A strong temperance sentiment prevailed in Taylors Creek Community, tho there were some lapses among the men, as drinking was then more or less general. Whether a man drank more than was good for him depended upon the individual and his environment. Within the sacred precinct of Taylors Creek nobody was ever coarsely and vulgarly drunk, tho one of its prominent citizens, or a popular scion of an important family might become slightly or somewhat "disguised in liquor," according to the prevailing euphemism.

One pretty social custom long gone into the discard, not being consonant with the glare of electrically lighted streets of even the rural towns, was midnight serenading. The young swains of the neighborhood serenaded their own sweethearts occasionally, but it was always a compliment extended to any visiting girl. It was all very romantic and thrilling to be awakened, perhaps in the wee small hours, by the tinkle of a guitar, the passionate moaning, or the dancing twinkle of the violin, the harmonious blending of low, intensive young voices in a popular love song, then, as the serenaders slipped away, the strains of "Home Sweet Home" wafted softly back. There was much pretense of mystery about the episode. One was not supposed to know the identity of the visiting musicians.

Amateur theatricals were all right in Taylors Creek, but with strange inconsistency the people there frowned upon the professional stage. The nearby city of Savannah had the oldest theater building in the whole country, it having been built in 1820. The large cultured class of its citizens furnished many eminent patrons of music and the drama. If your soul delighted in these things you would make trips to the city that you might enjoy the performance of a noted actor or the rapture of listening to some queen of song. It was well not to say anything about it after you came home. A theater building was regarded as some sort of profane temple, and anything that occurred there, tho all right in itself, was not to be commended. Such were the straitlaced views held by many otherwise tolerant individuals. They had not had the advantages of extensive travel, than which nothing is more broadening mentally. There were a few exceptions to this narrow-minded attitude, but they were very much a minority. With the class of purists there were four cardinal sins which today are among the chief forms of amusement of the socially inclined;

those sins were designated as card playing, dancing, theater-going and novel-reading. Oh, the times and the manners!

I must have been a precocious youngster owing to the fact, for which I am grateful to my parents, that they were rarely ever too busy to answer my questions and to explain in the best way they could the things I ought to know. There was no childish fear on my part in going to either of them. Words had for me a great fascination. Before the dictionary could explain itself to me I went to my mother for meanings and applications of strange words. I became a champion speller, largely because of the popularity of spelling matches when small boys and girls were permitted to enter into competition with older and more advanced students. To win or nearly to win in such a contest was to inspire ambition. I learned to read at an early age. There was not so much "literature for children" as at a later time, and the fewer books were, many of them, of a serious character. In those years war clouds were gatherings over the country, destined to break in all their fury. Political discussions among friends as well as on the public platform were growing more frequent. Many such discussions reached my ears. Things were said that I did not understand, but did not always forget and afterwards learned to interpret for myself.

The Doctrine of States Rights seemed to be growing more intense. I am not sure but that state pride was stronger than national pride. Personal liberty was much spoken of. It was a common taunt among children in their small disagreements, and even among the servants of the family—"You must think you are as big [smart] as the governor." I do not remember ever to have heard about the importance of being president. It was always the governor, I remember at a later time the visits of two governors to our city and that each time the celebration took on the air of a great civic and military pageant.

# 5

## WAR TIME AND AFTER

Another family migration took us to the city (Savannah). Viewed in the light of succeeding years, this was a fortunate move. The war was more nearly imminent than many realized. The Secession Convention was held the next January, and the state declared itself out of the Union, following the example of her sister state and immediate neighbor. I have called the convention the Secession Convention, for that was what it resolved itself into, but there were a few of the older men who were greatly grieved that there seemed no honorable way to remain in the Union. We had in our home as a guest an elderly gentleman, one of my father's friends, who was a delegate to the convention from an adjoining county. I remember him distinctly and the long serious conversations he had with my father and mother. I was too young to know the import of those conversations, but felt that they were of very momentous matters. Later, when I was old enough to understand, I heard my mother relate the circumstances of that time and refer to some things predicted by my father's old friend, which had come true.[2]

There was a lighter side to the visit of that old gentleman. He was a man of good presence with rather long white hair, which gave him a somewhat distinguished air. He was well advanced into sixty years. But for all that and his zeal for the welfare of his country, he must have had a sentimental side to his nature and a rather egotistical opinion of himself. At the time there were two friends for a sojourn in our home, one of them my mother's young sister, lately widowed, the other a young married woman. The old gentleman, a widower, must have been looking about for a young wife. He was a man of

---

2. A review of delegates to the convention from surrounding counties reveals this gentleman was Henry Strickland of Tattnall County. Ed.

substantial property and good social and political standing and probably reckoned upon that. He attempted to pay his addresses to my aunt, but was too blind mentally and physically to distinguish, between her and her friend. Late one afternoon he found his way into the parlor which, according to the custom of the time, was kept darkened. Seeing there one of the young ladies, who was the married woman, he mistook her for my aunt, precipitately declared himself and asked her to marry him. Though she could scarcely suppress her giggles, the girl realized the gravity of the situation and got out of the dilemma as best she could. Knowing positively that my aunt would have declined the offer, she decided for the gentleman's sake not to reveal to him his mistake in the identity of the two. She continued to play the role, discarded him as tactfully as she could and then rushed from his presence to tell my aunt and my mother of the embarrassing incident. After that when Mr. Strickland came to dinner, the two friends were supposed to be dining elsewhere.

A funny joke was told on this same old gentleman by the neighbors in his country home. There had been depredations committed upon some flocks of sheep in the community. A farmer had lost several sheep that had been killed by dogs. A "sheepkilling dog" has no right to exist, and when it is found that there is such an animal in the neighborhood all the dogs around are under suspicion until the killer is found. When found and his guilt is established beyond question, his fate is decreed, and tho the dog may have been of good character previously and highly prized by the owner, there is no setting aside of the verdict.

Mr. Strickland valued his dogs very highly and evolved a unique plan to discover whether any of them was the recent marauder. He had small bells attached to the neck of each dog. The following Sunday he went to church as usual. Hound dogs are noted for their social proclivities and their habit of making unwonted and unwelcome visits to the neighbors. On that particular day when the preacher was in the middle of his discourse a sound was heard afar off as of tinkling bells. The sound grew louder and directly there came into full view of the congregation from the open doors and windows of that country church, several hound dogs with noses to the ground, scenting a trail, yelping and baying as they came. Before one could know what had happened or could stop them, the whole number had entered the church and vociferously sought and found their master. Mr. Strickland with the help of some other men was able to expel Ringwood and Jowler, Hunter and the others, and to send them home in charge of his grandson. As the last dog departed with the boy, the old gentleman evidently feeling the effects of the encounter, looked up into the face of the preacher and said, "You may go on now, Brother Jesse." And somehow the church services were concluded.

The secession of the state was celebrated by a big torchlight procession the following night. The homes were illuminated. Tinners turned out as rapidly as possible little tin candlesticks with a sharp-pointed triangular base. After all curtains and draperies had been removed, the little candlesticks in great numbers were stuck into the wooden frames of the window panes. Most homes had windows with small panes of glass. A large house with a great many windows lighted in this fashion was truly a gay spectacle. The monster parade carried torches after torches, transparencies and banners, all led by bands of music. I surely remember that torchlight procession. It was not a declaration of war, but if war had to come, let it come.

Northern people sojourning in the South began at once to return home. One other incident I fully remember, the case of a little woman who called upon my mother for some purpose not now know, and tearfully declared her fear that she would not be able to secure a berth on a steamer before the blockade would be started, whatever that might lead to.

There was very much talk of war. The militia began drilling and parading the principal appearance. I heard them called "ragamuffins," a new word to attract attention for the first time heard.

There were several crack military companies in the city who also began parading and drilling. Their appearance was cheered on by the women who went to front doors and windows and even onto the streets to see them. Children with nurses were told by the nurses "that the boom-ba-lallies" were coming, and there would be great scampering to front doors. There was one artillery company in Savannah whose organization dated back to the American Revolution. This was the Chatham Artillery, one of their early cannon, and a sign of great honor and distinction mounted the top of the company's armory. Those were times of general excitement. Little children felt but could not understand the change in the air from previous quieter times.

I remember one night when everybody seemed under tension, as tho expecting something unusual to happen. There seemed a mystery in the air, the older people conversed very little, and that little was in low muffled tones as tho the walls had ears. Words heard then came back long afterwards with their awful meaning, "riot" "insurrection" "Negroes." There was dread of a race riot but it never came, owing perhaps to the wide firm action of the leading men of the town, the city officials, and the military.

Young men in great numbers were enlisting in the army. Preparations for war were begun. It must have been about the middle of April, 1861 when I saw across the street one grey morning a young man in military clothes, bright uniform and cap carrying a gun. I was at the window in my aunt's room when she was standing before the mirror combing her long beautiful hair. I went to her and told her what I had seen. She said that the young man was a soldier going to the war. All this was very vague to me. I had recently passed my ninth birthday. Many, many years have gone by since then, but I have not forgotten that first Confederate soldier in his bright uniform with his gun on his shoulder, stepping quickly along the street that grey morning in April, 1861.

So thoroughly was the doctrine of States Rights imbedded in the hearts and minds of the people, it was generally believed that the States would be allowed to remain peacefully out of the Union. Southerners had done their very honorable share in establishing the American government, and the two interpretations of the Constitution had always existed, so why not let the two sections divide if they could not agree.

I am not trying to discuss the War Between the States, as many Southerners prefer to speak of that terrible conflict, but only to touch upon some features which affect my story.

When war was declared after the bombardment of Fort Sumter, there was no longer any delay in trying to prepare for what was coming, even tho it was believed by many that the war would not last long. Camps were established and the work of enrolling soldiers went rapidly on. My mother's youngest brother, tho less than sixteen years of age, enlisted along with a friend a few years older. Other members of the family on both sides also enrolled. My father, Samuel Harn, was given a commission for an important and onerous undertaking, but one for which he was peculiarly fitted and which he fulfilled faithfully to the last of that four years' struggle. He was made purchasing agent for a large division of the Southern army. His duties took him out into the farming and stock-raising districts of a part of three states. Every kind of foodstuff and of livestock that could be converted into food for the soldiers he bought and sent forward from various shipping points to the army. He had a number of men, sub-agents, detailed under him for the work of driving the livestock to the distributing points and shipping to the army. As his immediate helpers, my father took with him two of his most trusted and intelligent Negro men. One of these men belonged to the early Negro families on the old plantation. In a way, my father and this Negro had grown up together. There was a strong bond of friendship between them, both before and after the emancipation, which lasted throughout their lives. They were born and died at nearly the same time.

After the richer farming and stock-raising sections had steadily yielded of their stores, it became necessary to make explorations out into the remote stock-raising districts where great numbers of cattle were raised on the free ranges, miles and miles in extent. Those districts were very sparsely settled, and long perilous journeys had to be made, mostly on horseback. In some places there were no real roads and no human habitations, and no food and shelter could be had, even of the poorest sort. Somebody had to find those ranges and then ride to reach the owners and pay for the livestock in Confederate paper money. This particular branch of the service could not be delegated to a subordinate. The paper money was worn in a flat padded roll on the person of my father and of his immediate body servant. Tho it seemed of not much value as measured by the gold standard, this money represented the faith of a people in their government and its integrity. Every dollar of its receipt and disbursement was rigidly accounted for.

From the cattle ranges to the railway station, boarding a train of any sort, riding night and day to reach a point, sending telegrams, and letters written from box cars; glad when permitted to stop off for a day or so to find a comfortable bed and something fit to eat, while he directed a sub-agent in some branch of the work. There were full four years of this, brightened by an occasional visit with his family, when by a considerable journey they could meet him somewhere during a brief stop-over on one of his routes, or, when a needed conference with a higher departmental chief brought him home for a short time. My father was intensely patriotic and put heart and soul into his work, sparing himself no hardship that fell to him in the line of duty. A man of great energy and ready initiative, resourceful, he accomplished vastly more than a man less mentally alert and physically rugged could have done. Much of this versatility was due to the splendid training he had received on the old plantation,—and he loved his fellow man.

The South had been an agricultural section and the people gave of their abundance as long as it lasted, doing without many things at home that the soldiers might not go hungry. They did go hungry, however, when supplies at home went low. The need for clothing for the Southern soldiers was another problem. The volunteer military organizations which had been established previous to the war had their own uniforms. These were not standardized, and, moreover, there was an age limit to them, more particularly as many of those uniforms were not adapted to hard usage.

Because of having been almost entirely agricultural rather than manufacturing in its industrial life, the South had become greatly dependent upon the North for manufactured goods. This was one reason why the Democratic party had championed lower tariff rates. The South by the blockade became cut off from foreign markets for its raw materials. The people went to work to remedy this. Blockade runners slipped out of Wilmington and Charleston harbors, taking with them great quantities of cotton for English looms. Sometimes the runners were captured, but when successful they brought back much in the way of medicines, military stores and luxuries.

There were many interesting historical happenings which, even then, I could comprehend, but those things are not pleasant to recount. I wish to speak of only a few salient features. Abler pens than mine have attempted to write the history of that period.

"It never can be told,
Tell it as you may,
The story of the glory
Of the men who wore the grey."

As the war continued and most of the Southern forts along the coast fell to the Northern forces, blockade running became extremely hazardous and was almost abandoned. Supplies from that source were finally cut off. Nassau, in the Bahama Islands, was the neutral port and mart in which the exchanges were made.

Some textile mills were established as early as possible for the manufacture of a crude wool and cotton product, notably one in Richmond, and one in Charlottesville, Virginia. In two cities in Georgia were factories which turned out a coarse domestic cotton on a considerable scale. Other states were doing the same. But these, with the home product, did not keep up with the demand, and Southern soldiers many times fought in rags and barefoot. The few shoe factories with their crippled resources could offer but a crude and limited output which fell far short of the need.

Much cotton and wool were made into cloth in all the country homes. The woods were hunted for dye roots. These with a few simple chemicals furnished the colors. Most of the carding, spinning and weaving were done by the women and girls of the family. The Negro women did not take kindly to the work. Many a delicate woman, the mistress of the plantation, had to labor to the limit of her strength to provide for the family needs; and the Negroes were kept in the fields at work or in the laundry, where they were at home. After the cloth was woven, it was made into garments. The Negro women could sew the coarse garments for the Negroes when cut out and the work explained, often many times over.

Grey was the adopted color for the soldiers' uniforms, a neutral color that blended well with the landscape and the smoke of battle. Besides, the agents for dyeing the material were easily obtainable in large quantity. Grey for the uniforms and the women's homespun dresses, grey for the jeans worn by small boys. "Butternut" for the Negroes. Men engaged in the prosecution of the war who were not in the ranks also wore grey. Much was accomplished by good tailoring. Some handsome suits were turned out in a smooth grey material befitting any man, but intended for long and careful wear.

Shoes worn by the people in the country were made mostly at home, often of leather cured on the home place. Cloth gaiters for women made from old coats and trousers were worn with pride. Black oilcloth, of the kind that had been used for the cheaper grade of carriage cushions, was made into children's shoes. My father had a pair of shoes made of alligator hide which cost two hundred dollars in Confederate money about the third year of the war, and were considered handsome.

It was not deemed patriotic to wear finery if you had any left. Garments were turned and made over for other uses than the original intent. Palmetto had many uses. Hats for ladies made of palmetto and trimmed with dried brown grasses were very pretty. In Jacksonville, Florida, for some time after the war, several ladies found lucrative employment in their own homes by the manufacture and sale of palmetto hats to the early Northern tourists.

One of the most interesting of the home manufactures was syrup-making. Many gallons of syrup and much cane sugar were produced on every farming place in the lower South. The syrup was usually of fine quality; the most that could be hoped of the sugar was a very light brown; the facilities for clarifying were not of the best.

In the way of food and beverages much economy was practiced, and much exchanging of recipes, for substitutes. A substitute for coffee greatly exploited at the present day is believed to be identical with the corn-wheat-rye "coffee" the Southern people used in wartime. It was not harmful, and when served with cream the taste was very palatable. What many of the Negroes called "simmon and sassafax" beer, was made of ripe persimmons and flavored with sassafras root, and was not bad. Indeed, that drink can be very nearly duplicated at any soda fountain at the present day.

Extensive salt works on the Florida Gulf Coast furnished salt. Ice from the North was cut off. Artificial ice invented by Dr. John B. Gorrie of Apalachicola, Florida, had not long been known, and was not in general use.

The skill and ingenuity of the Southern people was severely tested, but they did not complain if they could achieve results. If by any chance they could send a box from home to the soldiers of the family it was done. Homecured meat, molasses cookies, a warm homespun shirt for Bob or John or Bill, found their way into the box with a loving letter and scrawl from the child who had been left a baby at home. The posthumous child was always treated with unusual tenderness.

Who wants war? The Spanish American War was scarcely more than an incident in the lives of the American people as compared with the other wars thru which I have passed. That titanic upheaval, the Great World War, has no part in what I am trying to relate. The fratricidal strife between our own people was peculiarly harrowing. This war and its aftermath left a shadow on our Southern younger generation which time itself has hardly been able to lift thru the years that have passed. My father lost two brothers, my mother two brothers, besides other members of the two families.

Before the war, school facilities in our city were of a high order. I had been entered into a Select School for Young Ladies "Huntingdon Hall." When the war started this school was broken up. Other schools shared the same fate. Surely a calamity of the times! There had been "select" schools for boys as well as for girls.

Then it was discovered in this time of need that there was in the city a man who for some reason was not eligible for military duty, a trained teacher, originally from the North, a man of fine executive ability in his chosen profession. He had been brought South just before the war, at the instance of some farsighted citizens who wished to establish a good public school in the city. With the breaking up of the private schools came this man's opportunity. The new public school building was large and well equipped. Its doors were thrown open and the best class of citizens were asked to send their boys and girls there. Educated ladies of good social standing were the assistant teachers. The school soon had a paying enrollment at lowered rates, and with some others its capacity was reached. Those were democratic times. The school flourished and deservedly so. Curriculum, methods and discipline met the demands. The principal was a vital force.

Tho some may have doubted the sincerity of the man who had thus thrown in his fortunes with the Southern people, there was not long any cause for suspicion. If he harbored any disloyalty to the people, among whom he lived, he was never caught napping. This man, James F. Cann, spent his life in teaching, incalculable in value, which he did right there. He married into one of the city's best families. The sons of that union were later among the most honored men of the state. One became a distinguished jurist, the other a leading business man.

My brother two years my junior, and myself became for a time members of the school spoken of. We had all sorts of patriotic goings-on. The latest war songs were taught in the school. We had tableaux vivants suitable to the times. One day Mr. Cann requested me to go downstairs and bring from one of the assistant teachers a new war song. It was called "The Homespun Dress" was set to the tune of "The Bonnie Blue Flag," and soon became very popular. On my way back upstairs that day I nearly learned the first verse, and got laughed at for lagging.

My younger brother was scarcely of school age when he was placed in a primary school under a teacher, who, even now seems to have been a very excellent kindergartner; I am sure one of the very best I have ever known. If ever a woman was born to teach she was. As a young woman she had been widowed very shortly after her marriage under circumstances peculiarly sad. The rest of her life she devoted to the work of training little children. Everybody knew and loved "Miss Maria," Mrs. Maria Allen, niece of one of Savannah's oldest citizens, Mrs. John McFarland. There were always more applicants for places in her school than could be taken. I have looked somewhat into the kindergarten system of teaching since those days, and it seems that this self-directing woman must have had the same inspiration for her work as came to Froebel, tho, it is doubtful if she ever heard the name Frederic Froebel. All the best features of the best kindergartens were here, songs, plays, handiwork of various kinds, recitations, manners, morals, storytelling, legends, were all here.

The Christmas before the war opened there was a Christmas tree for the school. There were gifts for everybody and some set aside to be sent to certain poor children. In addition to the things on the tree, a number of plaster paris figures were given as special premiums. Those atrocities I fully believe had been bought as an act of charity from a miserable looking foreign street vender, who had been hawking about the streets great loads of the figures in a basket. They mostly represented birds and roosters with emerald green wings, vivid red toes and scarlet beaks, a hen of the same color sat brooding upon a dish that was supposed to be her nest, and so on. In honor of our little brother we two others had gone to the Christmas celebration and had each received one of the choice bits of art. Our return home with our treasures occasioned much merriment.

The war went on and proved a more serious and dreadful struggle than had been generally anticipated. Reviews, military parades, were the colorful features. The most thrilling and the grandest pageant I have ever witnessed was the review of ten thousand Southern troops by the Confederate General Beauregard at the military Park in Savannah in the early period of the war.

> "'Twere worth ten years of peaceful life,
> One glance at their array."

Our home was on a very broad street with a parkway thru the middle. Many a night we went to the windows and watched company after company move down the parkway in semi-darkness to the beat of muffled drums, marching to the railway station. I remember one regiment that waited part of a day in the railroad yards. The women of the city went with great loads of food which they served in the big cotton sheds and on the warehouse platforms. There we met my father's brother Tom. Dear Uncle Tom, genial, carefree and happy, he had always been fond of music and dancing and the social side of life. The regiment was on its way to Mississippi. We never saw or heard of Uncle Tom again, only that he was reported "missing" after the battle of Vicksburg.

One sorrowful recollection comes back to me of a day in April, 1862. Fort Pulaski, the nearest fort on the coast about twenty miles away was under bombardment. My grandmother was with us that day. Her youngest son, the boy then less than seventeen, was one of the garrison. All day long at regular intervals we heard the canon—BOOM-BOOMA-BOOM-BOOM. Hearts were full, tears flowed freely, but no one spoke much. The boy was not killed, but was taken to a Northern prison. A year later in the exchange of prisoners he was returned, an emaciated wreck with scarcely the semblance of a human being, to die in less than two weeks after.

After the fall of Fort Pulaski on our immediate coast, many people rushed to the interior as refugees. Whole plantations of Negroes were sent to the upcountry. Many of the white families soon returned when it was found that our chief danger lay north of us. We remained only a short time. The men of the family were away at the front except for a short furlough home at long intervals, and some came not back at all. We were more in the line of my father's going and coming but these glimpses were not satisfactory and otherwise we were better off at home, so we went back and stayed.

The war went on. There were many bloody struggles during the third year. Men and supplies for the Southern army were being depleted. Times at home grew harder. The courage of the Southern people has never been surpassed in the annals of history.

It was in December, 1864, the Christmas tide was approaching. In Savannah we heard about evacuation and pontoon bridges to cross the river as the remnant of that wing of the Southern army prepared to retreat before Sherman's advancing forces. The night of December 19th was a memorable one. The soldiers were crossing the river, the warehouses, with the food that should have been given to feed the more than half-starved Southern soldiers but had been withheld, were now thrown open to the rabble and looters. Throughout the next day the mob sated their greed. The night that followed was full of misery for the watchers. The mayor, Dr. Richard D. Arnold and the few remaining city officials had gone forth and proffered the "Keys of the City" to the advancing army and had asked protection for the city and its people, mostly women and children and old men too feeble to bear arms.

The next morning, December 21, 1864, Sherman's army took possession. The city was placed under military rule. Whatever hardships followed thru that time were the incidents of war, and we survived.

At last, at the end of the four years' struggle and it was admitted that the Confederacy had fallen and only the finishing touches were being put to the struggle in Virginia and North Carolina, the disabled soldiers and others out of the ranks who had struggled heart and soul in the work of furnishing goods and supplies for the southern armies, now started homeward. My father reached his home again. Footsore and weary, shabby and hungry, he had walked many, many miles. The Yankees had taken his commission from the Confederate Government which he would have liked to keep.

Because of the dangers attending a solitary man on foot he had to make his way by circuitous route. Plantations had been laid waste and abandoned. Negro quarters were deserted. There was one pathetic episode that filled my Father's heart with sadness when he

afterwards learned that on his brother's abandoned plantation old
Maum Rhina had been left alone. My father had spent the night in
one of the cabins believing that there was no other human being on
the place. The old woman had been left by herself until some of her
grandchildren could come back and take her away. She never saw
"Mas Sammy, my chile" again. Roadways were filled with stragglers
and also Union soldiers at the military post all the way miles out of
the city. As my Father neared one of those posts he requested to
be taken to headquarters, (General Kilpatrick's) where he asked for
protection. For the next few miles between that place and the city he
was not molested.

After the return from our refugeeing experiences, my mother
decided to place me in another school for young ladies. During our
absence a very excellent institution, La Retraite, had been established
by a lady of French extraction who had been educated in Paris. Her
grandfather had been a planter in the French West Indies during
the French Revolution. After the bloody uprising of the slaves in
the islands the family had gone to France. This lady spoke beautiful
Parisian French and utilized her accomplishment by making French
the language of the school. I had had a year or so of this school
when the vicissitudes of war caused a change in the personnel of
the teachers. The school was then taken over by a highly cultured
woman, Mrs. Henry Williams, daughter of the distinguished Judge
John McPherson Berrien. Mrs. Williams spoke French as her own
tongue and with the aid of one or two others conducted the school
after the December Holidays when martial law made it acceptable for
young girls to go unaccompanied upon the street. This school while
it lasted, which was only for some months, offered rare privileges for
obtaining a polite education for girls.

Among other vital questions confronting the Southern people
after the war was that of education. Many of the people were land
poor, but with business waking up again we had enough left that
city children could have the advantage of some teaching. The girls'
and boys' schools started again. The man who had made such a
success of the public school opened a boys' select school which was
in reality an efficient preparatory school. Not many young men could
look forward to a college career. Most of them had gone into the
Southern army at a very early age. They came back from their terrible

experiences as men. They had known but little of the happiness that rightly belongs to adolescent age. Now there were other stern duties to face in the rehabilitation of broken homes and fortunes. Many of these young men had to assist at least in the care of widowed mothers and sisters. But they had had some education and possessed good breeding, which after all is the one indispensable requisite.

The Savannah public school, so efficient for a time, had had varying fortunes during the last year of the war. The loss now of the man who had been the force back of it left it not much to reckon with. The need for a good system of public schools, a system maintained largely by taxation was realized. A charter was obtained from the state legislature granting local control for Chatham County. The first attempt at grading after the regular plan was then inaugurated. There was a small charge in the grades and the high school was made self-sustaining. About this time funds were available from the Three Million Dollar gift from the philanthropist George Peabody to aid education in the South. That sum, tho large in the aggregate, in the division was only an aid, but Georgia gratefully accepted her share.

Success attended the schools from the start. The Board of Education was selected from the best business and professional men of the city. The beloved Dr. Richard D. Arnold was the first president of the board. Wm. H. Baker became superintendent, Hugh F. Train and Bernard Mallon, principals respectively of the Boys and the Girls high school. When, a few years later, Mr. Mallon resigned and removed to Atlanta, he was succeeded by Mr. Wm. S. Bogart who had for several years conducted one of the most popular preparatory schools for girls. These men were all known for scholarly attainments and high moral character. There were other men, and women too, engaged in launching and maintaining the high standard of the schools. Their names are well remembered, but the list is too long to repeat here. They gave of the best that was in them. Improvement, development, expansion, marked its progress until the once small system of city schools is now a component part of a great state system of Education.

In that new organization of Savannah's city public schools, boys and girls were taught separately. For several years there was no co-education in the Protestant schools. Much was made of the individual and individual rights. It was only when the city public schools became a part of the state system that important changes were made. Previous to that time the two Roman Catholic parishes, Saint Patrick and the Cathedral, had their schools managed apart from the Protestant schools, and tho under the same superintendence, they had a separate curriculum and were largely governed by the Catholic clergy.

It was while the boys and girls were under separate governance that Miss Florence Bourquin was principal of the Barnard Street Boys school, a graded school of several hundred boys. As principal, Miss Bourquin was wonderfully successful. The Barnard Street school was one of the best managed in the city. At the present time there are many women of exceptional executive ability who are filling public positions of trust and responsibility and their work is taken as not anything unusual. But then it was different. That this little woman, brought up in the thralldom, (blessed thralldom), of Southern traditions could step beyond those traditions and not lose one whit of her womanliness and personal charm is still a matter of wonder and admiration.

Miss Bourquin assumed no air of spurious masculinity. She succeeded by sheer force of intellect and broad common sense. She had tact, firmness, and by intuition perhaps a sympathetic understanding of boys of the intermediate and adolescent age. No matter how recalcitrant or insurgent a boy might be by nature, Miss Bourquin could bring him across.

She possessed indomitable courage and faith in herself of the kind that inspires the confidence of others and brought to her much helpful encouragement. In the schoolroom she was the efficient executive, somewhat exacting in the requirement of fealty, but always just, and, as one of her pupils once said to me, "Miss Bokine would always give a fellow a square deal." Miss Bourquin, in the schoolroom; in the homes and hearts of her people, her juvenile charges,—"Miss Flo'ence." The span of her life was not long; she passed to her reward when she had scarcely reached middle age. The goodness and beauty of her life remains as a lovely fragrance with those who knew and loved her.

While Savannah was building up her system of public schools; in the country districts the people went back to the private schools, the only kind they had ever known. But some of the communities were so impoverished that little could be done for education. The boys fared even worse than the girls. After awhile some aid was granted from state and county, but for a long time was totally inadequate.

Soon, however, there was an awakening of economic life. Then both schools and colleges started on the upgrade. Magnificent agricultural resources lay undeveloped. Cotton came into its own again, and Cotton was King. Foodstuffs were raised for home consumption. Livestock anywhere near the populous centers was nearly depleted. Farmers knew that this was about the most dependable source of revenue and began to collect the scattered remnants of flocks and herds. The small farmer had the hardest time. Fields had to be circumscribed, everything possible in the way of foodstuffs must be produced at home, the family needs had not grown less and labor was scarce and high. But he did not falter, borne up by the cheerful assistance of his family. Women and children had learned much in an economic way during the war, which stood them in good stead now. Southern women who had not been obliged to work in the more prosperous times now hoed in their vegetable gardens, milked cows, made butter, looked after their poultry flocks; and such supplies as were not needed for the home table they sold to the nearest market. Even then women were beginning to learn the joy of being economically independent thru their individual effort.

During the period immediately following the war the freed Negroes had largely abandoned the farming districts for the towns. When it became known that the government would no longer care for them, large numbers returned to the farms and went to work to make a living, aided and guided by the white people. There was very little friction between the Negroes and the former slave owners, and there would have been practically none but for the scheming politicians and the thieving hordes who fastened themselves upon the South for what they could plunder and rob from the people and the government. When the people got back their birthright in the government, conditions rapidly improved, and the natural resources took on a new development.

In the rice-growing sections conditions were resumed pretty much as they had been before the war. The overseer was again in power as much as ever, perhaps. Daddy Primus or Uncle Peter was there too, in all his newly acquired dignity as a free man, but loyal and indispensable as ever. Rice was a crop raised on a large commercial scale and could be easily financed. Cotton too was a world commodity for which funds could be obtained. The great marts of the world were open to receive the crops as they could be sent forward. A giant industry was being developed in naval stores.

The so-called "reconstruction" period lasted for more than ten years. The struggle of the Southern people against the thieving politicians during that time was hard and bitter. At last, the people, the decent white people, came into power and the control of legislation. The year 1876 was marked by bumper crops all over the country, and the dawn of a better day came for those living below the Mason and Dixon Line. There were some ugly government scandals for a few years, but they were national in character. About this period some dreadful calamities happened in the North the result of which were felt indirectly in the South, but none of those happenings were as bad as the South had passed thru in the closing time of the war—not even Black Friday, the financial crash of 1873, the Boston fire, and the great Chicago fire. The South had learned to endure, and after endurance came the revival of hope—faith and courage had never failed them.

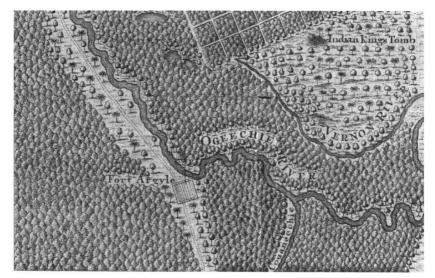

This section of a c. 1735 Savannah map by Tobias Lotter and James Oglethorpe depicts the Ogeechee and Canoochee rivers as well as Ft. Argyle. The fort helped protect the Savannah-area settlers. Many Bryan County land grants just west of these rivers were ancestral lands of the Harn family. (Courtesy of Hargrett Rare Book and Manuscript Library, University of Georgia.)

Rice culture was important during antebellum times in Bryan and surrounding counties. The Harn family grew rice on their Ogeechee River plantations and to a lesser extent when they moved to their Canoochee River land. (*Harper's Weekly*, January 5, 1867, private collection.)

In Julia Harn's sketches, she describes customs and characteristics of slaves in Bryan County. After the Civil War, groups of African Americans from Savannah's surrounding environs traveled to the city to sell their produce and wares. (*Harper's Weekly*, May 29, 1875, Savannah Public Library, Gamble Collection.)

Julia Harn recalled the Savannah market: "The structure itself was a large open building with a strong heavy, arched roof, with massive supporting pillars. The area beneath was divided into stalls and open compartments for the various kinds of food, meats, fish, dressed poultry, vegetables, and bakers' products." (*Harper's Weekly*, May 7, 1878, Savannah Public Library, Gamble Collection.)

Julia Harn attended the renowned Taylors Creek School in the late 1850s and this Liberty County institution is vividly described in her sketches. Pictured is the original school building which burned in 1930. (*Taylors Creek 1760 – 1986*, Wyman May, et al.)

Taylors Creek c. 1940 after the U.S. Army acquired it as part of the area for Ft. Stewart. Julia Harn's family moved to this settlement in Liberty County about 1858 for mercantile business interests of Julia's father and the opportunity for the Harn children to attend the highly regarded Taylors Creek Academy. (Courtesy of Vanishing Georgia, Georgia Archives.)

Julia Harn recalled of the Confederate soldiers in Savannah during the war as, "reviews and military parades were the colorful features. The most thrilling and grandest pageant . . . was the review of ten thousand Southern troops by Gen. Beauregard at the military park in the early period of the war." (*The Soldier in the Civil War.*)

As Julia Harn described Savannah's fall, "The next morning, December 21, 1864, Sherman's army took possession. The city was placed under military rule. Whatever hardships followed thru that time were the incidents of war, and we survived." (*Harper's Weekly*, January 14, 1865, private collection.)

General Robert E. Lee paid
a final visit to Savannah in
1870 on a tour of the South.
As students at Savannah's
Chatham Academy, Julia
and her classmates attended
a meeting with General Lee.
As Julia later described it,
they had an opportunity to
"pay our respects" to the distinguished general. (Courtesy Library of Congress,
Prints and Photographs
Division Washington, D.C.,
LC-USZ6212658)

Julia Harn taught at Massie
Public School in Savannah on
Calhoun Square for a number
of years beginning in 1873.
The building is the only remaining structure of Georgia's
original chartered school system. She later taught in several
locations in Florida and briefly
managed a business college in
Gainesville, Florida. (Courtesy
of Massie Heritage Center,
Savannah, Georgia.)

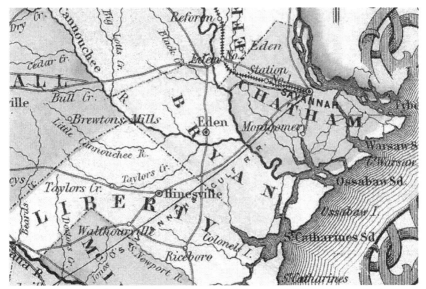

This 1855 map of Savannah and surrounding counties to the west shows the Canoochee River section, Taylors Creek and the two railroads serving the area. (J.H. Colton Map of Georgia, 1855.)

Georgia was the leading state in the South for producing lumber during most of the antebellum period and Savannah (pictured) and Darien were its busiest seaports. Timbermen rafted logs through rivers to the ports where the squared timber was loaded on ships for transport. The income provided by the forest industry was important to the economy. (Courtesy of Vanishing Georgia, Georgia Archives.)

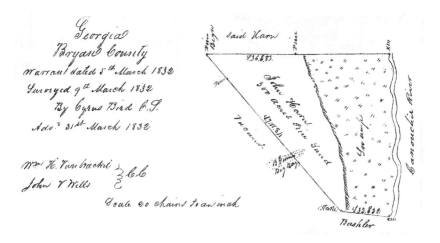

The Harn family acquired thousands of acres through purchases and land grants in the Ogeechee and Canoochee river areas during the 18th and 19th centuries. The above plat is of land acquired by John Harn through a headright grant. Julia spent her early childhood years on "the old place" near the Canoochee River. (Courtesy of the Georgia Archives, Deed Plat Book AC.)

This 1950s Canoochee River photo shows a Ft. Stewart landing. The river is central to much of Harn's writing. The stream begins in Emanuel County and flows southeastwardly through or as a boundary of Candler, Evans, Bryan, and Liberty counties. The Canoochee traverses Ft. Stewart and joins the Ogeechee River from the west in Bryan County near Kings Ferry about 12 miles from Savannah. (Courtesy of Vanishing Georgia, Georgia Archives.)

Julia Harn is pictured with her brother, Samuel P. Harn. He died at the age of 23. This photo was likely taken in a Savannah studio during the period the family lived in the city. (Courtesy of Special Collections, Lucile Hodges Papers, Zack Henderson Library, Georgia Southern University.)

Julia Harn in her 60s. She said about her historical writing, "These scenes are typical, and the manner and customs are true as they prevailed . . . . These are the things I remember from my own life, sidelights of those old days. If these glimpses of the faraway time have charm to stay the reader's attention, my purpose has been well served." (Courtesy of Mary Ann Cofrin.)

E. Merton Coulter (1890–1981) was a professor at the University of Georgia where he was chair of the History Department for 18 years. He was editor of the *Georgia Historical Quarterly* for 50 years, and also published numerous books. Though they never met in person, Julia Harn and Dr. Coulter formed a cordial relationship when he agreed to publish Julia's articles in the *Quarterly*. (Courtesy of Hargrett Rare Book and Manuscript Library, University of Georgia Libraries.)

Teacher, historian and author Lucile Hodges (1906-1995), of Claxton, Georgia, attempted to have an edited version of the Julia Harn sketches printed in the 1970s. Although her compilation was not published, her research was extensive. Miss Hodges described Julia's work as, "A valuable reference and commentary on the times about which she wrote." (Courtesy Special Collections, Lucile Hodges Papers, Zack Henderson Library, Georgia Southern University.)

This 1942 photo provides a view of the Ogeechee River. In the mid-1700s Julia Harn's first American ancestor, John Harn, moved from his Ogeechee home to his new lands near that river's confluence with the Canoochee. His former land later became part of Henry Ford's plantation at Richmond Hill. (Courtesy of Special Collections, Lucile Hodges Papers, Zack Henderson Library, Georgia Southern University.)

The left side of this photo shows the mouth of the Canoochee River where it joins the Ogeechee. Julia Harn spent her early childhood on her father's plantation a few miles away near the Canoochee River. Julia describes the watercourse: "The river itself was alluring; beyond the call of its beauty, it offered easy transportation to the seacoast, an important advantage at that time when there were few if any roads into the wilderness." (Photograph by Dr. Curtis Hames, Jr.)

# PART TWO

# *OLD CANOOCHEE BACKWOODS SKETCHES*

## 6

## OLD CANOOCHEE PLANTATION

We called it "The Old Place," and a beautiful old place it was, that old Canoochee Plantation—in the big bend of the Canoochee, the pretty tributary of the Ogeechee River, and not far from the confluence of the two rivers in southeast Georgia. The Canoochee found its source in the lower foothills of upper Georgia. In its later course it ran nearly parallel to the larger river until after the latitude of Savannah was reached, then turned east and joined the Ogeechee on its way to the sea. In this lower Canoochee valley there was just one large landed estate, which extended some miles along the left bank of the river into a forest of long leaf pine, oak, hickory, and trees of lesser growth,—wild cherry, dogwood, redbud, and wild grape vines. It was truly a sportsman's paradise, filled with many varieties of wild game in its primitive state.

This plantation had been the home site of the family for more than a hundred years. The Colonial ancestor, John Harn, had come into this favored region in the late 1740's, bringing with him his wife, nine sons and daughters, and a group of twenty-nine indentured servants, from his old home in Scotland. That was in advance of the introduction of African slavery into Georgia in 1749. Because of the indentured servants, this ancestor, "immigrant" as the original Colonial settlers were called, was able to obtain a greater acreage of land than was permitted under the earlier land laws. The indentured servants were succeeded by Negro slaves in smaller numbers, perhaps, while many of the more worthy acquired land for themselves, and were aided in becoming useful and honorable citizens.

The plantation proper of this Canoochee estate comprised only a relatively small part of the landed area. The home was located about a mile from the cove of the river and nearer to the highway which in a general direction paralleled the river. The cultivated fields were manned by Negro slaves, no great number of Negroes, just enough to lend interest to the general activities of farm life where the master was his own overseer and rode his own fields to direct operations.

The place in its nearest direction was twenty miles from Savannah. The soil was fertile and well adapted to the farming that was carried on. The chief source of revenue was cattle-raising on a large scale. It was a general stock farm. Fine horses, cattle and even pedigreed dogs were the features of the home life. The big woods held a wealth of the finest timber, always available when wanted.

The original dwellers of the plantation had passed thru the vicissitudes of the period just before, during, and after the War of the Revolution. The first John Harn was an ardent and active patriot. The early settlers suffered much from the Royalists of that time as well as from invasions. Those who committed depredations against the property of the patriots under the claim of loyalty to the British king were known as Tories. The name as applied and those who wore it were held in contempt ever after, down to the third generation.

But all those troubles were now past. Ranking among the gentry and financially independent, the old plantation family enjoyed prestige and material comforts beyond what was known to many of their less fortunate neighbors. This, however, had no effect upon the spirit of neighborhood friendliness. Life was peaceful and happy, and for the time was untroubled by the storm clouds that were beginning to show upon the political horizon because of the question of State's Rights and African slavery.

Just beyond Canoochee Plantation and extending along the river, was a somewhat thinly populated district of small farms and settlements. The people of this backwoods were the descendants of a sturdy British yeomanry, who also had come there just subsequent to the Oglethorpe period and in advance of the American Revolution. Those early settlers had left the immediate seacoast, and had been lured into this interior by the magnificent timber and the abundant native grass. The river itself was alluring; beyond the call of its beauty, it offered easy transportation to the seacoast—an important advantage at that time when there were few if any roads into the wilderness. The small farms as established were in a lesser way the replica of the larger plantation in the variety of its activities,—some general farming, large cattle raising, with timber as an extra source of revenue.

Cattle raising was carried on by free ranges. It had not yet been found necessary to restrict the grazing of cattle on free ranges, as in more populous communities. There was, of course, some regard given to the ownership of lands. The public lands of which there were large areas, were entirely free for grazing; but grazing on private property was by permission, and the grazing did not include any other form of adoption. Wild lands were rarely posted. Hunting of wild game was without restriction. There were certain ethical rules and a gentleman's agreement among sportsmen which all right-minded men were supposed to obey.

Only a purely wanton individual hunted for the pleasure of destroying wild life. If such a one showed himself, he was made to feel the disapprobation of others and was likely to be publicly reprimanded.

Along the Canoochee River with its forests of magnificent pine, timber was an important asset. For many years Georgia "heart pine" had a name and a prestige in the big lumber markets. As confined to the Canoochee section, the business consisted in the cutting and floating of sawmill logs to the city of Savannah, where, because of its excellence, the timber commanded an exceptional price. The route by which the timber was taken to market was by rafts from the Canoochee into the Great Ogeechee River to the sea; then up the coast between the sea islands to the city. This was a much favored route when the weather was propitious, but in the season of storms was attended by great hazard. The records show very few fatalities, but there was the ever-present danger in any rough weather of the loss of the timber and the men being blown out to sea. In the earlier part of the 19th century, the Savannah-Ogeechee Canal was built to eliminate the dangers and to shorten the distance between the two rivers. However, the sea route had its lure for men of adventurous spirit, and was not wholly abandoned by those who rode the rafts.

The first settlers of the Backwoods beyond Canoochee Plantation were a strong, upstanding people, who cared little for the pomps and vanities of life, a rugged class, as they had to be to endure the hardships of their pioneer life. Their descendants had inherited much of that ruggedness. These later ones had not greatly changed their mode of living, but had continued in the same old routine handed down by their forbears. The domestic regime was much the same. Whatever prosperity had come to them was not greatly evidenced by any improvement in their home life. In the near-by city of Savannah there was an aristocratic element who had acquired and practiced the art of good living. In the city homes and on the plantations there was an excess of Negro servants, each of whom had been trained to render service that promoted the ease and luxury of their masters. The absence of Negro slaves in the backwoods left everything to be done by members of the family.

The men liked to count their herds, the women counted their poultry flocks; and this far in excess of what would have been expected from the lack of conveniences in their homes. The backwoods people were inured to their cheerless homes; they had never known any better. What had been good enough for their ancestors was good enough for them. They lived much in the open and were generally healthy and happy. The farmers raised at home nearly everything they needed in the way of supplies, the cotton and wool for clothing; the leather for shoes was largely produced on the place. Only the better shoes and clothing was bought in the city. It was a common saying that the farmer lived at home.

The Canoochee backwoods was typical of other sparsely settled interiors where the people were of the same original nationality and had developed along similar lines. Throughout the early Colonial period Georgia had been settled by groups of diverse nationality, each of whom held rather closely to old family traditions and perpetuated certain racial characteristics. However, with changed economic conditions in the new world, there came about in urban centers and the more populous rural sections, a gradual merging of interests that worked to mutual advantage. The backwoods people largely held aloof from the changing influences. They were independent and happy in their own way. They rather scorned urban ways and were a law unto themselves. This certain kind of independence may have been a saving grace to the backwoods people. Anyway, it entitled them to respect.

# 7

## NATIVE CHARACTERISTICS

The African slavery introduced into Virginia shortly after its settlement spread to all the Colonies. Even the most sincere and tender-hearted philanthropist could see nothing wrong in taking a savage and converting him into a more or less decent human being, even if it were necessary to purchase that savage from his so-called master. The experience having been tried by them, the people of the Northern states soon found that the African Negro was not adaptable for any branch of skilled labor, nor was the extremely different climate adapted to the Negro. The very best thing was to get rid of him. In fact it was an economic necessity to let him go. But where did he go and what became of him? It is in the province of those who know, to answer that question.

All the Southern slave holding states had rigorous laws governing the presence of free or freed Negroes in their midst. There were a few Southerners (when nearing the end of their time), who realized that the ownership of slaves was undesirable, and set free those who had served them. One freed Negro among a lot of slaves could exercise an incalculably bad influence. So, whatever did or did not become of the Northern freed Negroes, it is an absolute certainty that no slave-holding Southern state opened its doors and welcomed large numbers of them under the status of a free people. In the setting aside of slavery in the Northern states, some Southerners saw the opportunity to increase their slave holdings. The inference is plain that Negroes who entered any of those states did so in diminished numbers and under government surveillance, or they came in as any other property bought and paid for.

Violent agitations of the slavery question were started over the country, with which this little story has nothing to do. The pages of history have recorded the workings of the whole matter.

Canoochee Backwoods was a typical backwoods community. The people there owned no slaves nor did they covet any. The Negro was an outlandish creature for whom they had no liking. Any Negro would have been treated humanely, even kindly by them, but he would have been in the way. Canoochee Backwoods was not opulent enough to establish the slavery system within its confines, and the ownership of one or two slaves would have been unwise. Requiring separate living quarters, quite beyond the family circle, the Negro would not fit in with the domestic scheme. Negroes are intensely social; where Negroes were held in family groups and treated decently, as they generally were, they were a happy carefree people. The personal and social condition of one or two Negroes isolated from association with their kind was pitiable. It was like keeping a wild bird or a wild animal in close and solitary captivity, and seemed cruel indeed. Canoochee Backwoods had no need for the Negro.

It was characteristic of the average backwoodsman that he liked to employ primitive methods in whatever he did. He did not take kindly to new-fangled ways; he liked no methods conforming to any set rules other than had been practiced by his forbears. He pursued a straight line of action, and when a thing was done he gave his mind and body a rest, and did not waste any mental effort in vain speculations upon abstract subjects. In this he was as far from the man of academic mind as the poles. He translated his thought into action.

The backwoodsman was the product of his environment,—the seemingly illimitable wilderness, the vast unpopulated expanses, leading on and on, and beyond. He did not like close confinement in any way. It was expansion, freedom he desired, freedom to live his life in his own way, not trammeled or hampered by too many conventions.

Yet he was a law-abiding citizen. He paid his taxes; served on the jury when called; did his duty as a citizen on the public road (worked the road or paid for it); voted at the election for his favorite candidate; and was ready to help to the very limit of his ability and knowledge in an emergency. The backwoodsman was hospitable to individual strangers, but held at a distance any "furriners" who could not give a clear and understandable account of themselves. He was clannish and did not readily take strangers on their face value; he was easily suspicious of people he did not know. To those who felt it worthwhile to cultivate his confidence and did secure his friendship, he was loyal to the last ditch.

He reckoned himself in manly attributes the equal of any man. He stood on his own platform, and feared no man living in what he had to say; but if he thought it good policy he could be as discreet as the sphinx, and felt it no hardship to ride all night on a secret errand of importance to himself or his clan.

The main business of the backwoods was farming and cattle raising. These lines of work were carried on after the manner of long ago. The traditions of the earlier settlers were rigidly adhered to. There may be better methods practiced at the present time which were unknown then, but this rule holds everywhere, and the backwoods farmer of that time may have done as well as others in the prosecution of his affairs. If he sometimes hit upon a better way than he had previously known, the discovery was his own and did not come from the schools. There were then "Country Gentleman" and "Farm and Fireside" magazines finding their way into the homes of the farming people, but these as yet had no clientele in the backwoods, where there was but little time given to reading. The backwoods family subscribed to and read the nearest weekly newspaper, which they sometimes derisively characterized as the "Blanktown Excuse" because of its poor quality in every way, but of which they would not have liked to be deprived. There was no R. F. D. (Rural Free Delivery) service then. Everybody had to get the mail—which may not have come oftener than once a week—at the post office. It gave one a small distinction to have the newspaper come addressed to John Doe, Esquire, or to Mrs. Richard Roe.

The Family Bible and the yearly almanac held a conspicuous place in the "hall" (the front living room) of every home. The almanac was frequently consulted for weather predictions and for notes on farming, and time for planting the garden. One famous old almanac had its astronomical calculations made by one of the early scientists; the name of the almanac was "Grier's Family Almanac" and held the place of honor, in name at least, long after the very old Mr. Grier had passed on.

The older backwoods people read the Bible religiously every Sunday, the others less often, perhaps. But even then they could quote from the Bible certain things (aphorisms and maxims for living) which many close students of the sacred book have failed to discover within its pages. Much that was figurative they accepted as literal in belief but not in practice—like the injunction "If thine enemy smite thee on the cheek, turn the other cheek." Many good people would have been shocked at any other than a literal rendering of much that they read. The Old Testament history they interpreted in terms of the present. The dire predictions against the wickedness of certain of the ancient Jews which had been visited upon the offenders, and the punishment that had been borne by them very long ago, were believed to apply directly to the people of this time, were yet to be fulfilled, and were "signs of the times" which indicated the near approach of the Millennium.

Those good people observed the Ten Commandments as nearly as they could in their daily living. If there were any noted lapse it was in the Third, but that was a very general lapse. There was at that time much profanity among men in all walks of life, even among men in high station. Perhaps the way to account for it is, that in times of great stress and storm they had called upon the Almighty for help and it had been given them. They realized that this was the one sure hope in time of trouble. The God of their fathers had never failed them. To that one familiar source of succor they had resorted. Perhaps from this familiarity had come an easy form of speech which had developed into irreverence that had spread, and with the spreading the irreverence had grown into gross and general proportions. By instinct the backwoodsman was reverent. He lived close to nature and it made him reverent.

Because of their outdoor life and their work with the cattle and the calling of the dogs, the men were loud-voiced and clear of speech; but the women were very gentle in manner and low voiced in a drawling musical way. Many of them bore beautiful names, drawn from the classics and from early British poetry, which had been handed down thru many generations. Family names too, indicated British origin. Many legends, old ballads and traditions held their place in family recitals. Ballads of the days of chivalry, and ballads of the old Border Warfare, were still sung to the same old tunes. Many

old expressions and old sayings could be traced back to the time of
Shakespeare, and many superstitions also. Speaking of superstitions,
not all the beliefs so classed were anything more than scientific facts
for which no body could give any reason. Many of the older men had
lived very close to nature all their lives, had observed her moods and
variations and had learned many of her secrets. They had observed
the moon's phases, the influence of moonlight as well as sunlight
upon growing plants. The moon ruled the tides, why may it not
influence other natural phenomena, and in large measure determine
the time for planting certain crops?

Taken all in all, the life of the backwoods, while uneventful
held the charm of serenity and quiet contentment for its people, a
permanence of family life that is not so much known at this day.
Many a backwoods home has thrown its stabilizing influence around
its children in the formative period of their lives and has sent forth
its sons and daughters who have been reckoned among the finest
citizens of the land—men and women who have not been ashamed
of their backwoods origin.

The boys had their outdoor interests dear to the heart of any
boy. They learned to ride from the time they could sit upon a horse;
at eight and ten they had bird traps which they set in the field when
the crops were off. Game of all kinds was so plentiful there were
no legal restrictions as to decoying, trapping or shooting other than
those founded upon ethical principles as to the seasons and times for
such pursuits. The bird traps were made of sticks, usually pieces of
shingle tied together with strong cord. The sticks were placed one
upon another in crisscross fashion and were built up so that the trap
would be a few inches higher in the middle and large enough for two
birds. The trap being strongly bound with cord, was then set upon
the smooth ground and the "setters" placed. These were three sticks,
one to hold up the trap, the other two at the slightest touch would
throw the trap to catch the unwary bird that had entered under it for
the grain sprinkled there.

Usually at twelve the boy was given a small shotgun with which
he soon learned to shoot birds and small game. When he was fourteen
or fifteen he could go with his father and other men on their hunting
trips. It was the ambition of every boy to bring down some specimen

of big game. If he did, and the game was a deer, the antlers were hung up in the hall as a permanent trophy of his skill.

The children were given their animal pets. Sometimes it would be a hen and chickens. In that case it might be necessary when the chickens were weaned, to cut the end of the small toe for identification. It would not do to clip the long central toe nail, that was what the chicken used in scratching for its living, but the tip of the small toe was all right. Now the rule is to band the leg of the chicken for identification. Little children nursed puppies and puny pigs. When they did not die—which the pesky things frequently did in spite of the care given—and they reached adult age, they brought much pleasure to the children.

Girls early learned to spin and sew and knit. They were often married in their middle 'teens, so the girls usually started at ten or twelve to furnish their hope chest. Of course, you know what a "hope chest" is; it is something every woman knows about and cherishes. It is a chest or trunk containing things—table and bed linen, pieces of "fancy work" and fine needle craft, which the girl will need in her home after she is married. Her women friends often add to the stock of useful and pretty things. At one time the girl had to begin early to make her patchwork quilts and to spin for the articles she would need, hence the name "spinster" applied to an unmarried woman.

In these modern days when styles and fashions change so often few girls try really to fill a hope chest; instead, her friends give the engaged girl approaching her marriage, "showers" or parties, and literally shower her with gifts. The bridegroom's friends also contribute to the showers as well as to the wedding proper; and since "All the world loves a lover," every friend and invited guest feels obliged from sentiment to make as beautiful and appropriate gift as possible. Customs change as much for the times as for the different grades of society. The backwoods friends and neighbors were as sincere and kindly as any in their friendship for their young people.

The farmer's girls were often assisted by their family in some enterprise that would bring them spending money. Perhaps they raised spring chickens for the city market, or turkeys for Thanksgiving or Christmas and New Year's trade. The girl may have been given a cow of her own.

The children were the most interesting feature in any backwoods home. They showed the effect of their wholesome outdoor living in robust health and a usually happy disposition. Every family could boast of from five to ten or even more boys and girls; and each child born into the family was welcomed as a heritage from the Lord, and they grew up in that happy atmosphere. Family devotion and clan loyalty were marked characteristics of the backwoods people. There was sometimes a feud between unrelated families, but never any such thing within one's own family.

The habits of thrift and industry found imperative by the early settlers had been established and passed on down to their children. But the regular fixed habits of work that were known by the backwoods families were not really so rigid as to impose hardships on the children in any well regulated home. The parents themselves lived up to the belief that "All work and no play makes Jack a dull boy." This easy philosophy so ruled their lives that almost any farmer or his wife would willingly set aside a piece of work to have a little impromptu picnic or to go to visit some of their kinsfolk or neighbors. This rule was followed by the best of them.

Truly there were some in the neighborhood who were lazy shiftless, pretending to trust to the claim of luck to hide their short-comings. If Farmer B had an exceptionally good crop because he had worked toward that result when the lazy man was sleeping or loafing, the lazy fellow declared that Farmer B had extra fine luck in whatever he did. When Mrs. B had a fine garden and a flock of chickens that she was bringing to a profitable marketable standard by close and unremitting care and labor, the shiftless, lazy woman whined that she herself never had any luck in anything, seeming to forget that she had not done anything to deserve any especially good luck. For that reason Mrs. B because of her extremely good luck was expected to furnish the other woman's family with "greens" and other things which the woman could easily have cultivated at home.

Perhaps it was the spirit of mutual helpfulness and interdependence in which they had grown up, thru the necessities of living, that made the members of the average household so kindly thoughtful of each other. The father was the head of the house, the mother came next in authority; the father dealt with the sterner matters, the real business and government, the mother with the softer side, to whom the children went when they wanted a certain sort of sympathy which could not be described, but which mother knew all about.

It was inevitable that in large families there would be cases of discipline to be dealt with by the father. In these the mother rarely interfered, except in private; to have done so openly would only have made matters worse, beside being wrong in principle. If the father lost control of himself, or was unjust or cruel, the mother at no matter what cost to herself would interfere in behalf of her own child. Family discipline was rigorous in those days. It was allied to the religion which some people held and which bore traces of the gloom of the Middle Ages. Instead of regarding punishment as a restraining influence against wrongdoing, there were many individuals of that time who believed that punishment—which meant some sort of personal infliction—was a just and righteous thing in itself, to be dealt out to offenders for the slightest infraction of what was often an arbitrary ruling of some one or more persons in authority.

There were parents brutal in the exercise of authority over their children. Much of this proceeded from pure narrow-minded ignorance, and as men became more enlightened discipline became milder. It may be urged that the pendulum has swung too far in the other direction, and that there is but little parental government in the homes of today. Perhaps that is true, but is not the present condition a reaction from that earlier time? Laxity on the part of parents has taken the place of that old severity. There is a wise and happy medium by which children may be protected against their own weakness and inexperience—guided not driven and left in possession of their own souls.

In Canoochee Backwoods there were few if any domestic tyrants. If a man who was supposed to be the head and reasonable governor of his family became habitually harsh and cruel to his wife and children, he was made to feel the disapproval of the entire community. It was extremely rare that any disintegration of the family occurred. The backwoods woman had been trained both by the traditions of her family and the outer circumstances of her life to endure. Because of this and her pride and shrinking from making her unfortunate family life a matter of common knowledge, she often endured what no self-respecting wife is now expected or encouraged to endure in silence and tears.

In the same way a good man may have made an unfortunate marriage, but he usually made the best of it. He may many times have been embarrassed by the idleness of his wife and the inefficiency of her so-called housekeeping. Often that man was good-natured, a pleasant, happy sort of fellow. If so, he really had the best of it. His friendliness and good nature under trying circumstances bridged over many an embarrassing situation. His genial philosophy was contagious. Neighbors were attracted toward him. Tho the dinner may have been badly cooked, the rooms disorderly, the children not so clean as they should have been, he was too loyal to his wife and family to appear to notice. Perhaps he would excuse himself to a visitor for a short interval when he saw the smallest child approaching, and take the child aside and surreptitiously wash face and hands, hastily slip on a clean dress if one could possibly be found; then the baby child (with or without a clean dress) was presented by the father with a proud, "Isn't he a fine fellow?" A man or woman with such a nature is a blessing to know.

## 8

### JOHN BENTON

One of the finest men in all Canoochee Backwoods was John Benton. John was not without his faults, but his virtues and his lovable qualities far outshone any faults. John was half poet, half philosopher. He loved nature and the big outdoors. He loved the song of birds, the glint of the red bird's wing; the glimmer of sunshine as it sifted thru the trees and fell upon the dark pools of the creek where the fishes hide; the white sand banks in the river when the water was low; the old mill site and the great sheets of water that tumbled over the big wheel. On moonlight nights he sat up late and talked, because he loved the moonlight. On dark nights, soon after the sun had gone down, he went to bed and slept. He arose in the early morning, long before the sun, at the time when all the earth was wrapped in beauty; and as the sun came up over the rim of the earth every bush and leaf sparkled with dew or hoar frost. That was the time when Chanticleer dropped down from his high roost in the treetop, and mounting the nearest fence sent forth his clarion call to the rising day. All the young creatures, the hen with her brood, the puppies, the kittens, the pigs, the young calves in the barnyard, joined in the morning chorus.

These sights and sounds were a joy to the soul of John Benton. He was happy, he loved his wife, the sweetheart of his youth, the mother of his children; he loved his children, each child in turn, but the baby, the last of the brood, a little more for the time than the others. John had always honored his father and mother; it would be little short of high treason to fail in any degree of love and reverence to that old mother now that his father had passed on and his mother was bereft of much of the happiness of former days.

Though John Benton loved his wife, he was master of his household. His wife followed his wishes as nearly as possible. From his children he exacted strict obedience. There was no deviation from his orders, and little or no wrangling over a matter. To someone looking on, this arbitrary way of dealing may have seemed hard and unreasonable, but the family had never known any other rule of living. John had started in on the very first day of his marriage to pretty and timid Mary Willis, who was very much in love with him, and she had acquiesced in his wishes. Since that day they had got along as well or better, perhaps, than most married couples—there was no wrangling.

The one thing that made John Benton an agreeable man to live with was that he was no grouch. If he didn't like a thing and thought it worthwhile to say so, he spoke pleasantly, and the correction was made. There was no scowling or grumbling, no black looks and hateful or ominous silence. The incident was disposed of, was dismissed, and that was the end of it. Thru the day neither wife nor child shed a tear or gave a sigh over the trivial happening.

In the very beginning of their married life John Benton had told his wife in his quiet way that she could mind her own business as she saw fit, and he would hardly interfere; but that he was "goin' to 'tend" to his own business himself, and didn't want "no woman interferin." He didn't want too much advice unless he asked for it, and no questions nor suspicions as to what he was about. Married life begun on this philosophical plan had lasted more than twenty years and had moved serenely and happily. Mary Benton had unbounded confidence in her husband, in his wisdom and his love. He had always provided for his family as he had said he would, and they had lived comfortably if not plenty of hard work for everybody, but each one knew what was expected of him. John attended to affairs on the outside, and there was rhythm in the household under Mary's guidance.

There were times when John ordered a halt in the day's work, and the whole family occupying the big farm wagon would go to the river and spend the greater part of the day, fishing, lolling and resting. After the bountiful lunch that Mary and the girls had hastily but amply prepared, the whole crowd again climbed into the big wagon and went over to Bill's. John and Bill had been friends since they were children; perhaps John had not seen Bill for a week and wondered what he was doing. That evening the family reached home in time for the boys to feed the stock and finish any other small jobs about the home. In that part of the country they never spoke of "chores." The word drifted down to them later.

# 9

## FAMILY LIFE

The life of a backwoods woman began—and often ended—early. Married while still in her early teens, she assumed the cares and responsibilities really designed for more maturity. It was truly the survival of the fittest. The physically strong, vigorous woman who had been bred to her fate, may have welcomed the hardships of her life, but there were many who succumbed. Often there were women of thirty who looked old enough for their own mothers.

The round of daily duties began in the very early daylight and lasted with but little intermission until well into the night. There was always a large family to provide for, with breakfast by candle light so that the men and boys could get to their work in the cooler hours in summer. The same routine was held to the rest of the year for one reason or another. In the farming season the men came from the fields when it was too hot for any outdoor work, which was always before noon. They rested then, ("nooned") until time to go back to work, generally about an hour or so after the midday meal.

If the farmer was the right sort of man, he and the boys (there were always boys in the family), would go to the cowpen which was often some distance from the house and do the morning milking. The cows had to be milked early, before the dew dried, the cows turned out and the calves put to pasture. If he was the right sort of man, the water pails in the kitchen would be filled from the deep well from which the water was drawn by a heavy windlass and rope, or by a double chain and pulley. The old well sweep of earlier days had been replaced by these later mechanical contrivances.

After the breakfast was over the table was to be cleared, the dishes washed, and the pots cleaned, besides giving the little children their breakfast. Sometimes there was an older girl who could assist with these duties, but if the baby cried the mother's care was imperative. Perhaps the same small-sized girl could sweep floors, and if tall enough, help to make the beds. The shoes and other belongings of the men and boys had to be picked up from where they had been thrown and put in the right place.

Fresh vegetables had to be gathered for the dinner. The peas, beans, corn and potatoes, whatever kind was wanted, had to be brought from the garden or the "patch" a small journey away. Milk had to be strained and put away as soon as it was brought in. Later, the cream must be skimmed and the churning done. This was a big job in itself. The churning in the summer time was carried on under the big tree out in the backyard, when there was not so much difficulty in getting the butter to "gather" as in the winter. But under the most favorable conditions the poor little child wielding the heavy dasher of the big wooden churn would often grow weary and call for the mother's help and sympathy. When the butter had come the child's work was done. The butter then had to be taken from the churn, all traces of milk removed, and the butter moulded and put on the cool dairy shelf. The buttermilk was drawn off and set aside. Then came the tug of war with the washing and scalding of the various vessels and strainers, scalding and frequently scrubbing the churn, and putting all those things on the top of the fence where the air would dry and "sweeten" them.

All the varied ingredients of a good dinner—and each mother's son of those in the field felt that he was entitled to a good hearty dinner by reason of having earned it in the sweat of his brow had to be brought and assembled from variously separated locations in the backyard—from the smokehouse where the meats were, from the storeroom, the sugar house, the dairy. The cooking was done on a wide kitchen hearth, well equipped with heavy iron pots, usually of generous size; with racks and iron bars on which to set those iron pots; and with the big iron ovens and "spiders" in which the baking was done by placing fire both underneath and on top. The heavy lids of those baking ovens were lifted for inspection within by means of a long flat fire-stick. There were coals of good hardwood, oak or hickory, for any toasting. What was known as a spit was an arrangement for roasting before a bed of coals a large fowl—say a big dressed turkey (or a pair of ducks) hung by an iron hook, with a dripping pan beneath to catch the juices. There was a frequent turning and basting of the fowl to insure just the right degree of uniform brownness and tenderness.

It must be confessed that food prepared under these conditions did have a superior flavor, but it was a laborious way to get results. It required much skill in regulating temperatures, and much bending and heavy lifting by the cook. Think of it! Old as was the use of cooking stoves, their introduction into the Southern backwoods has been of comparatively recent date. Any town house not now equipped with gas and electricity for domestic use in not considered a worthy home.

The backwoods woman who lived in those times needed strong vigorous health. The daily cooking, cleaning and sweeping, the weekly, or even tri-weekly, scrubbing; the regular weekly washing and ironing—and where there were children, as there always were, it called for more or less daily launderings—all these domestic activities, even under favorable conditions made one strenuous round.

For the woman who had toiled ceaselessly all the morning, there were afternoon duties as well. When the noonday dinner was over, and the dishes, the pots and pans had been washed and scrubbed and put in their rightful places, there may have been a breathing spell when she might sit instead of standing. This was the time to darn, mend, and perhaps sew a little, which must be done by hand. Clothes for the men and boys were made at home. Sometimes two women who were neighbors would plan their work and take an afternoon off when they would combine their efforts in the cutting and sewing of garments. If there was a woman in the neighborhood who was considered a good tailoress, she might by some means be secured to assist one whose talents lay in another direction. As in the farming, harvesting, and building carried on by the men, there was a spirit of mutual helpfulness which worked for the general good.

At rare intervals some woman neighbor would come for a short afternoon visit and to exchange the neighborhood gossip, good or bad. This made the time pass pleasantly and speedily. When the neighbor had left, there were the chickens to be fed and looked after for the night; the evening milking to do, and "supper to fix"; and the children who had had more or less care through the day now came for an extra share. Soon the tired men and boys would be coming home from the fields and as hungry as tired.

If there were any children to wash the supper dishes, the mother would sit and rock and sing the baby to sleep, while the children did the kitchen work; otherwise the work must wait. That baby must be put to sleep in the way the good Lord meant it should be—in the mother's arms, quieted and soothed by the slow movement of the rocking and the low sound of her voice as she sang some favorite old hymn. This little respite from the cares of the day when the baby's bedtime came, was a boon to the tired mother as well as to the little child. This backwoods woman was one of the saints of the earth—an old fashioned mother.

### Marriage[3]

Marriage was the only vocation open to women of that time. Failing that their lives became a blank. In those days "ladies" did not go out from home to work anywhere in the South, and in the backwoods there was no compensations whatever for loss of home and family. In the more refined and cultured circles a woman who wished to live her life alone rather that enter in to an uncongenial marriage, was permitted to do so. Note that they were permitted, but there was little approval given to that course of action, unless the woman was possessed of an ample private fortune, which, of course gave a different aspect to the question. While men were clamoring for personal liberty of thought and actions-for political rights, the status of women remained practically the same as it had been for a very long time.

The so-called "Woman's Rights" movement was led as a forlorn hope by a few women, brave souls (!), who felt the economic as well as the social injustice under which women were living. Very young women of the present day can have no conception of the restrictions that were placed upon women only two generations ago. "Woman's Rights" as a name was followed by other terminology, "Suffragettes" and "Feminists" were names applied to those who joined the crusade. But the long-drown-out agitation has culminated in granting to women the elective franchise, the right, and moreover,

---

3. This section on marriage comes from the Julia Harn papers at the University of Florida. George A. Smathers Library, Department of Special Collections, Manuscript 73.

the opportunity to earn her own living if she has or wishes to do so. It has coerced women to be declared the equal of man in any profession or any line of business not limited by physical strength or physical endurance.

In those old days there were just three ways that a woman financially destitute could earn her living. Women might teach, but only a very few had education enough for teaching; there were a few "mantua-makers" and milliners, but the demand for them was limited even in the larger towns. Women "who sewed in families" were either on charity or else nearly on starvation. Women could take boarders, (now it is "Paying Guests") and literally work themselves to death. That sort of employment appealed more to women of social nature; and for women with children to care for it offered about the only thing to save them from absolute charity.

There was sometimes a man who did not like to see women work, that is really work. If the woman was a member of his family it was painful to him to know that she was without means of support. That man would offer the shelter and protection of his home any indigent kinswoman of even a remote degree of kinship to himself or his wife. If his wife was also kind and thoughtful in the treatment of the kinswoman her lot was a pleasant one; otherwise the poor relation had a sorrowful time. It goes without saying that any self-respecting woman would rather earn her own living than accept charity from any one, tho it should come from a near relative.

There was another type of man who took care of his "female relatives" in order to protect the family name and his own standing family name, forsooth. He failed to realize that the name was patronymic and not exclusively his own possession.

## 10

### FAMILY WASHING

In the mild climate of the lower South the family washing was usually done out of doors the year round, by selecting bright days in winter. In every family backyard was a commodious open shelter under which the worker stood. In the more primitive households deep troughs hollowed out of a length of tree of several feet, with an auger hole in one end with a corncob stopper was used for a tub. In addition, there might be a pail or two and one or two big iron-bound tubs made by sawing across a heavy hardwood cask that had originally been appropriated to some other use, perhaps it had been a syrup or molasses barrel. There was a heavy wooden block at a convenient height of two and a half or three feet, and a hardwood stick. These were the "clothes block" and the "battling stick" used for pounding the clothes instead of rubbing on a washboard. A huge iron pot or boiler stood on its own legs nearby. For convenience this equipment was placed not far from the well.

There was one rigid requirement that altho the trough, the tubs and the big washpot for boiling, could be conveniently reached from the well, no water, no soapsuds drained from the trough, the tubs, nor any from the pot, could be poured near, but must be carried to a safe distance to be emptied. Every family prized a good well of pure water; for not alone the comfort but the health of the family depended upon the purity of the drinking water. So, it was in a spirit of self defense that the people took care of their wells.

When washday approached, usually on the evening before, the soiled garments were shaken out, assorted, and the white clothes put to soak in cold or lukewarm water. The next morning as early as the other work would permit, the washing was started. And here again the help of the boys and men had been acceptable,—in filling the big pot with water and providing wood for the boiling. Then the real work began. The clothes were washed, soaped with plenty of good homemade soap, put to boil, taken out, pounded with the same big stick that was used to keep the clothes moving about in the pot; washed again, rinsed, wrung out and put to dry. There were no clothes wringers, and this was the very hardest part of the whole operation,—the clothes had to be wrung by hand. Where there were no clothes pins, and there generally were none, the clothes were hung on the cleanest part of fences, and on bushes to dry. The more enterprising homes had clothes lines. Before the wire clothes lines came into use there were small sized ropes, but they had to be taken down and put up frequently to prevent mildew and too early wearing out.

The question of personal cleanliness and the problem of how to remove dirt from soiled clothing is as old as civilization itself, and has come down to the most recent times. The laundry method of the backwoods housewife had much to recommend it. She had the advantages of good soft water, plenty of good clean homemade soap, plenty of wood for the boiling; and for the drying, clean sweet air free from all impurities, and sunlight in clean open places. The baby's clothes, the men's best shirts, and the women's best dresses were generally done at the same time as the starching and ironing.

The smoothing irons (anciently known as "sad irons") were the old fashion kind used from time immemorial. They were placed before a bed of glowing coals on a clean swept hearth, and when hot enough to suit each kind of fabric were polished to extra smoothness with a piece of beeswax or on the branch of a green pine top. As each piece was ironed it was seasoned before the open fire in winter, or in the open sunlight at other times. This old, old, method brought good results.

The weekly washday was the hardest day of the whole week for the housewife. In the average backwoods family everybody realized this and more or less consideration was exercised. The men and boys knew not to expect the usual big boiled dinner. The noon meal would be a quick meal or a lunch. But with the many good things from the dairy, the smokehouse, and the storeroom with probably some of mother's fine lightbread, which had been baked the day before, nobody fared badly. The boys and girls made jolly over the situation, the boys wanting to help "big sister" who after all was not so very big, but had been helping mother as best she could, while "little sister" had taken care of the baby. Between the two girls the dish washing and the churning had been done; and mother had stopped from the washing to help with the scalding of the milk things and had put them up high to dry. Father was thoughtful and had helped to carry off the used water from the trough and the tubs. And so it was a good day after all.

## 11

### HOME MANUFACTURES

In the back nook of every kitchen of every Backwoods farmhouse there was an ash barrel or hopper. This was made by taking a strong barrel (not a cask), boring holes in the bottom, and filling the barrel with oak and hickory ashes taken from the big open fireplaces. The barrel of ashes was set upon a slightly inclined platform, on which cleats had been nailed lengthwise.

From time to time water was poured upon the ashes, and after dripping thru was caught in a receptacle under the edge of the platform. This strong lye was used for making soap and for other purposes. When the time came for making the soap, the refuse fat which had been saved for this was put into the big wash boiler, water added, and boiled awhile. Then removed and strained thru a coarse cloth or sacking, was returned to the pot. Lye was added and the whole boiled the requisite time, which was determined by testing in a clean white plate. If hard soap was wanted, a piece of rosin, or even a piece of dry pine gum was added to the boiling mixture, but for soft soap this was omitted.

While the soap was boiling it must be stirred continually in one direction and by not too many individuals. Whether the manner of stirring had anything to do with the quality of the soap is not definitely known, but every good cook knows that fine cake batter should be beaten with firm steady strokes or by a cake beater in the one direction, to produce a cake of fine, smooth texture. Soft soap of a jelly-like consistency was put into a tight keg and put away. The hard soap was left to cool in the boiler; after that it was cut into bars, laid on a board in crisscross strips to harden. The soap made in this way was wonderfully good and cheap.

Spinning and weaving were among the necessary activities of every backwoods home. Girls of twelve were often the main dependence for the spinning; the weaving was done by the older women of the family. The unit of weight for the thread was the ounce. This was computed also for the cloth, and the comparative weight of all cotton, cotton-wool-mixed, all-wool and nearly-all-wool, as in the weight of blankets. With the simpler weaves of cotton almost any housewife could adjust the warp in the loom, but often the services of another woman who was particularly skilled in the work would be required to put in a piece of cloth—that is arrange the thread and determine just the order of procedure. Many of those women were good, even skillful designers of patterns for the beautiful wool counterpanes. Their designs were often the standard designs brought from the Old Country by an ancestress, but there may have been some that were original with this later woman descendant.

Those backwoods people must also have had some knowledge of dyeing the simple colors. The indigo growing all about them was the common source of blue; but besides the logwood black and the indigo blue, the patterns of the counterpanes were marked with a beautiful red, yellow and brown. All those colors were lasting, as could be shown by the very last remnant of one of the counterpanes. The cotton jeans for men's and boys' summer suits, various checks and stripes for women and children's dresses and aprons; plain white of different weights for different purposes—all these could be included in the summer output.

The greatest achievement by any home weaver was in the fine gray jeans for men's and boys' suits, the nearly-all-wool fabric for winter wear. Some of this goods was quite fine and handsome, being of smooth fine texture, and distinctly grey and uniform in color. When properly tailored those suits were worthy of much admiration.

Much of the weaving was done in the late spring and early fall. Some of the log houses did not have glass window panes and light was essential for the work. For the same reason it could not be done in the winter. It may be too, that a moderate temperature was better for the manipulation of the threads. Also, this time was when the chickens and gardens did not require so much attention and there was opportunity for cutting and sewing.

Knitting was another of the women's steady occupations. Nearly if not all the socks worn by the men and boys were homeknit. But this work was often done by the winter fireside; and if there were any women in the family who by the infirmity of age or weakness were not able to assist in the more robust duties, they did most of the knitting—which included-not only socks, but scarfs and wraps for women and children; gloves for the young girls who liked to protect their hands when engaging in the rougher duties; and "galluses" (suspenders) for the men and boys.

# 12

## FAMILY DOCTOR

The family doctor always lived a long way off in a more populous community, and was not available whenever wanted. It was necessary, therefore, that someone in each household should know what to do in ordinary cases of sickness, without depending too much upon the doctor. There were no long distance telephones, in those days, no automobiles, no hard-surfaced roads leading any-and everywhere. It was a very distressing but not infrequent experience to send a messenger some twenty miles away for the doctor only to find upon arrival that he had been called twenty or more miles in the opposite direction, and with no certainty as to when he would return.

So the best thing to do as a rule, was to guard the family health in every way possible by taking preventive measures. If there were symptoms of any ailment or sickness coming on, try to stave it off. If this could not be done, there were certain preliminaries that the doctor always prescribed in advance of any other remedies; learn these and be prepared. In case of accident, for instance, a broken arm incurred by a child falling from a tree, there was nearly always someone available who could set the limb correctly. And it had to be done without the aid of an X-ray since there were none known then.

In extreme cases the patient might be taken to the doctor, whose home office was something of a family hospital. People in cities were the ones who patronized hospitals. Many surgical cases as well as other forms of illness were treated in the home of the patient. Trained nursing as a profession was little if at all known, altho there were many practical nurses who had large knowledge of the work. Much of their knowledge was gained from the practice of rules laid down in a book known as *The Family Doctor*. More than one skilled practitioner had written a guide book for heads of families.

A book of this kind was in nearly every intelligent family, was the exclusive property of the mother and wisely withheld from publicity, but available to those who could rightly interpret its teachings. The lessons were straightforward and easy to follow. It was a treatise on physiology, hygiene, care of infants, and much extended and valuable information as to the treatment of simple maladies. This knowledge was primarily intended as intelligent guidance for mothers in the care of their families, and when ailments were of the common kind. In this there was no attempt to rob the regular doctor of his prerogatives, but to be a help in time of need—"To know what to do until the Doctor comes."

Besides the medical guide, there was always in every neighborhood, an elderly woman, herself a mother, whose services were vital in their importance, but strange to say, those very women upon whom the lives of mothers and children depended, were considered more of a necessary evil than a blessing. Tho next in importance to the surgeon himself, she was only somebody's "Granny."

Some knowledge of the healing art had been handed down in certain families thru several generations, and was highly prized and guarded. Medicines from the vegetable garden, and from roots, plants and bark found in the woods and old fields, were more or less skillfully compounded. Simple chemicals were produced—potash from hardwood ashes; iodine from weeds; iron from scales beaten out on the blacksmith's anvil. Manufacturing chemists now offer ready for use much that in former times, the chemist in the drugstore found only in crude form, something to be worked out by slow process. Many materials for dyeing the cotton and wool for spinning and weaving had also to be found in the woods. These were fixed with simple chemicals.

# 13

## INTERIOR TRAFFIC AND TRANSPORTATION

In addition to the means of transportation afforded by the natural waterways of the several rivers that found their way to the sea along the Georgia coast, there were certain highways leading out from Savannah, which even in that earlier period offered fairly good right-of-way for the traffic of the state. There were the Louisville and Augusta road, the Dublin road, and others that were a continuation of the Savannah-Ogeechee road to Kings Ferry, fifteen miles from the city. One of these was the Darien road, leading from Kings Ferry, south and west for fifty or more miles and terminating at Darien on the Altamaha River.

Darien was one of the first Colonial settlements of Georgia, dating back to 1734. It was settled by a group of Scotch Highlanders, brought over by Oglethorpe with the double purpose of founding a colony, and one that would be a military barrier to the hostile Spanish on the south. It may be stated in passing that the Scotch Highlanders proved themselves equal to all that had been expected of them both as citizens and as soldier patriots. The Darien road was built by slave labor after the introduction of African slavery. It was a broad stagecoach highway, much of it of corduroy structure through the swamps and lowlands. The road was well maintained for many years, until it was absorbed into the modern highway system of the state.

Another road from the Ferry junction led along the lower Ogeechee through the peninsula of Bryan Neck, and skirted the big rice plantations along the river. The story of those old plantations, their settlers, and the beautiful names they gave their places, many of them in remembrance of the old British Homeland, is truly a charming story, but does not belong with this sketch of the Backwoods, though only a few miles away.

A very important highway from the Ferry extended west and northwest into the interior of a thrifty farming section which the railroads had not yet penetrated. This road locally known as the Hen Cart Road, furnished the outlet from farms more than fifty miles from Savannah. Great wagons, sometimes caravans of wagons, loaded with cotton, wool, and all kinds of marketable farm products were a feature of traffic. Big wagons loaded two and tree tiers deep with all kinds of live poultry went to the city by continuous route and brought back supplies of merchandise and manufactured goods. Each wagon was drawn by an adequate team of horses or mules. Food for the teamsters, provender for the draught animals, and water for the entire number, had to be provided for in advance of setting out on the trip.

Along this highway were driven by slow stages to the city market large numbers of livestock. Some of the cattle were brought from as far away as the adjoining state of Florida. The cattle needed skillful management while on the trail. There was the further responsibility of knowing before setting out that the cattle should have water and food; and if possible, some grazing places along the highway. It was urgent that the journey be so graduated that advantage could be taken of the creeks and tributaries of the larger rivers, where the cattle could be forded across without danger or loss. The care of the vehicles was another item. Provision must be made against accident, so the necessary tools were taken along. Each of those big farm wagons had a container, a little pail or can of axle grease, dangling from the lower frame, for without the aid of the axle grease the journey could not be completed. When the weather permitted, most of the travel was by night, the resting in the day.

The teamsters and cattle drivers on the regular route had camping places, changing from time to time as the native grass became exhausted. The "cow boy holler" and the cracking of their long whips could be heard a far way off, and were a friendly signal when approaching a home in sight of the highway. Then everybody rushed to see, and to answer the signal, keeping a little back from the noise and the dust.

In those early days before there was such a network of railways over the face of the country, the travel along the highways was heavy. The stagecoach took care of much of this and provision was made for passengers at the relay stations. There were many private conveyances of various kinds seen on the roads. The wealthier class of people generally traveled in their own carriages, and sometimes with their servants and luggage following in another vehicle.

Something like a revival of the stagecoach days has come about in recent times judging by the immense travel of passengers by Bus (omnibus), and freight by truck lines. The contrast, however, is in the system of magnificent roads and the increased number of great national highways that extend over every part of the country, in substitution of the electric motor for horses, and in electrically-lighted and more recently air-conditioned railway and bus coaches, roomy and comfortably furnished. These changed and added features contribute pleasure rather than discomfort. In the earlier time a long journey was looked forward to with more or less dread because of the privations it entailed. The railways changed most of the uncomfortable features, but the railway then was often far away and not easily reached. It is a far cry from the sort of locomotion known to dwellers in the most advanced sections of the country less than a hundred years ago, and what is common today—from the oxcart and the covered wagon of the plainsmen, the American pioneers and frontiersmen of the early nineteenth century, to the airplane through the gradations of steam and electricity. These and the manifold discoveries and inventions of modern science—including radio communication, make this a marvelous time in which to live. Mother Shipton's prophecy has been fulfilled almost in its entirety.

### The Cracker Cart

One unique type of vehicle was the Cracker cart, popular with the small farmers because of its cheapness and its adaptability to varied uses, and its durability. The cart was often used as the family carriage, even to town, and for hauling small loads about the farm. It was built by the local blacksmith and wheelwright.

The original idea of the Cracker cart may have been borrowed from the Spanish settlers in Florida, or wherever early American settlers came into contact with them. The cart had only two wheels, and was built on the principle of the dumpcart. The broad wheels with rims several inches across were banded with heavy iron tires wrought in the blacksmith shop. The spokes and other parts of the wheels were hand-wrought of hard-wood, the body of simple and somewhat crude construction was fastened to the axle by strong iron linchpins.

The horse was saddled and the shafts drawn over his head; a broad leather band was carried under the horse's body and fastened to the shafts by sturdy wooden pins on each side. The saddle without stirrups was made secure. Instead of leather traces, small iron chains were used. Two-wheeled carts have been in use from time immemorial, but where the Spanish idea comes in is in having the driver sit in the saddle and guide the horse with the bridle rein—*a la* Spanish volante, whose coachman wore livery and carried a long whip. The driver of the cart with feet firmly implanted on the shafts gave added security. But it was a crude and ludicrous position for a man, and that is probably the reason that the boys, even the small boys on the farm, usually drove the cart, with feet resting easily upon the shafts. The father was far more at home on horseback, feet in stirrups, free and untrammeled, racing through the woods with the dogs following in full cry, both man and dogs rushing full tilt after game or stampeding cattle.

The name Cracker came from the cowboys, who used long plaited whips when driving the cattle. The whips were generally home-made, and had long strong handles covered with buckskin, and a buckskin cracker on the end. From long practice the cowboys had become expert in the use of the whips: the loud sharp crack of the whips, accompanied by the "Cowboy Holler," "OO-OO-OOO-OO," was thrilling and carried a great distance. The cowboys were known as the "whip crackers." The name was extended to include the entirety of the Backwoods people, who were nearly all engaged in raising cattle on the free ranges. Thus Georgia became known as the Cracker State. Both Florida and Georgia backwoods people are known as Crackers, even now, although the name has lost its significance largely. The cowboy holler was developed into the Rebel Yell which was used by Southern soldiers in the Civil War.

In the city of Savannah, as in many of the older cities, there was a large central market where all kinds of fresh food and vegetables were exposed for sale. The City Market in Savannah was located in one of the open squares for which the older city was noted. The structure itself was a large open building with a strong heavy, arched roof, with massive supporting pillars. The area beneath was divided into stalls and open compartments for the various kinds of food, meats, fish, dressed poultry, vegetables, and bakers' products. Immediately surrounding the structure on all sides, was an iron rail that guarded the low platforms where the hucksters disposed their wares. Great baskets and flat trays made of strong grasses, were piled high with tempting fruits and vegetables.

In this market the country people, mostly small farmers who could make trip from home in one day, would come to sell their surplus in the morning of the next day. In a part of the older city of Savannah, which once had been a residential section and was only a few blocks from Market Square, was an area of vacant lots, more than an acre in extent and enclosed by a high board wall. This was the Wagon Yard where farmers could park their teams for the day or night. A long, open shed furnished stalls for horses. In the open space wagons and teams found room. A large furnished house in connection with the wagon yard, afforded respectable quarters where the farmers or their families could lodge. However, as the lot might not be free of molestation, in spite of the police protection, the farmers and drivers occupied the wagons and carts to protect their own property. Most of the vehicles had covered tops.

Farmers going to market usually went in groups. Neighbors found it pleasanter if not safer not to camp alone on the return trip, which was frequently necessary. The neighbors would start from home in the early morning, meet by appointment at a convenient place, at the Ferry or the bridge, and travel in company, stopping near "Old Man Sineath's" place, which was the best for the noon-day lunch. Anybody who has ever traveled the Savannah-Ogeechee road from the city to the twelve mile post, long remembered the Sineath family and the great deep well with its springs of pure cool water. The hospitality of that homely little Dutchman, Peter Sineath, and his family in keeping that well by the roadside was as fine and pure as the water itself. The farmer group would reach the city in the early evening, and after a night of some rest would be ready the next morning.

Illuminating gas was used in Savannah at that time throughout the city, in public buildings, stores, offices, and in many homes until displaced by electricity. The city market, which had been less brightly lighted in the earlier night was brilliantly illuminated shortly after midnight. Butchers, bakers, truck gardeners, hucksters and venders of every sort would be coming in and getting ready for the early morning trade. The coffee stalls and lunch stands would be open. The farmers with country produce would also be there in the early morning light. With the horse hitched at a convenient rack not far away, the cart would be drawn up in front of one of the hucksters' platforms, with all the good things held back in the cart until the customers came.

City people then visited the market for delicacies that are now found in other places. Men, connoisseurs in food, and housewives, would appear in the early morning, followed by a servant with a large covered market basket, to select from the first offerings of the day. Many farmers had regular customers. They brought, as the season came round, fresh country butter, homemade cheese, sausage and various meat puddings from the recent hog-killing, fresh pork, dressed poultry, fresh eggs, game, venison, wild ducks, and wild turkey. The farmer women who sent their good things to market knew the value of appearance. Everything was beautifully clean, and there was a display of white cloth wrappings that was very attractive.

The merchants around Market Square confined their trade almost exclusively to the country people, and catered to their especial needs. Those merchants were not the regular cotton brokers. The latter had offices on The Bay, the river front. Cotton was stored temporarily in the great cotton sheds and warehouses in railroad yards and on the water front. But the Market Square merchants did a thriving business, nevertheless. In the exchange the farmers sold to the merchants barrels of cane syrup, cured meats, bushels of dried corn, dried peas and animal hides. A bale of cotton or wool might figure in the transaction. What the merchants offered in return represented staple supplies. Some farm implements, harness and other leather goods, farm and garden seed, horse blankets, canvas and cheese-cloth for crop covers, coffee, the finer grades of sugar, and the cheaper and coarser grades of shoes and dry goods. Nearly always the farmer received a suspicious-looking big jug that might or might not contain vinegar. Those jugs were more in evidence just before the Christmas Holidays, or in advance of a political rally or a barbecue.

### The Peddler

One of the honored institutions of that far-away time was the itinerant merchant, the peddler. Mr. Jasper Sims who as a young man had gone a volunteer soldier in the war with Mexico, and had come back with the loss of his right leg to his home in Canoochee Precinct, found that he must take up some other vocation than farming. Mr. Sims was a very active man, of lively temperament, with a keen sense of humor. He was withal something of a philosopher, and he loved his fellowman. These qualities admirably fitted him for the business of itinerant merchant. So, at the start, Mr. Sims fitted up a light spring wagon with a top for protection from the weather, harnessed his one horse, and went to Savannah, where one of the best merchants agreed to finance the enterprise and to furnish Mr. Sims with all the goods he would need for his country trade.

The initial trip proved financially successful beyond what Mr. Sims had anticipated. After that he went regularly. The jingle of the bells on the peddler's wagon, a noise sometimes further enhanced by the rattle of tinware, was heard with pleasure by the housewives and the children of the Backwoods. The former were much amused and entertained by his jokes and gossip, the latter were delighted with the candy which Mr. Sims never failed to remember. Mr. Sims studied the wants of his customers; he jotted down certain requests, and rarely was any one ever disappointed.

For the goods he brought, this traveling merchant received his pay in butter, chickens, eggs, and any other commodity in the way of country produce that the housewives had to sell. In the season when the men and boys had animal skins to dispose of he would make regular trips for the dressed skins and hides, coon, deer, dressed buckskin, pelts of otter and fox, and squirrel skins. The larger cowhides the farmers took into town as they did the cotton and cured meats.

There is an old legend that used to be told sometimes in Savannah to the effect that the ancestor of one of the largest wholesale drygoods merchants in the city had been a peddler who went from house to house in the more populous country-side with a pack on his back along dusty highways, alone and on foot only as he might be offered a ride by someone driving the road. He had come as an immigrant lad, a foreigner ignorant of the English language, to America, the land of opportunity. By the time this man had reached middle life he had laid the foundation of the ample fortune which later he had left to his children along with the legacy of a respected name.

## 14

### SCHOOLS

There were then in every populous Southern community flourishing private schools, and in every state many secondary schools and academies and some colleges, of high rank. But there were no public schools. In the thinly settled rural communities educational facilities were very meager. A common school term consisted of a "quarter" of three months, and woeful to relate, one such term a year was all some communities had, and the school term had to be pitched at a time that would not too greatly interfere with the work on the farm.

Since there was no regular public school system and no officials, in the backwoods section, the selection of teachers was an irregular matter, usually left up to the teachers themselves. The man or woman who desired to teach in a rural community announced the fact and went around the neighborhood with a written contract and secured signatures from the heads of families as to the number of "scholars" they would send. Sometimes a public meeting would be called at the schoolhouse to discuss and decide matters. If the number of pupils warranted, there might be a second teacher. While the salary was necessarily small and paid at the end of the term, the price fell rather heavily upon large families. But as a whole, the people were stoutly opposed to what was known as free schools; they thought that such a system, which they did not understand, savored of charity.

The question of transportation of pupils was not one of very serious consideration. Many of the boys and girls walked three or more miles to the log schoolhouse. When there were several small children in the family there might be some sort of conveyance provided, but that was rare. In those days people did not disdain to walk; it was considered good for them. The daily session opened about eight in the morning, or possibly earlier. There was a noon intermission, and school had to be "turned out" in the afternoon in time for the children to reach home before dark. It was often a jolly crowd that set out from the big log schoolhouse, talking, laughing, singing, wrangling, and swinging their dinner pails. Now and then there might be a scrap on the way that would call for later investigation. As a rule, however, the presence of a large boy or girl would keep down trouble. Years after that time, the question would come up for discussion in a gathering of teachers as to the extent of the teacher's jurisdiction over pupils on the way to and from school.

This may be said in favor of those old-fashioned schools: that if only a few subjects were taught, there was thoroughness. Methods took care of themselves; the brighter pupils had no limitation put upon them by being yoked to the dull or mediocre. Very much depended upon the educational qualifications rather than upon the professional training of the teacher. Many a bright boy or girl received intensive training in some favored subject because of the teacher's special knowledge of it. The worst handicap was the lack of books and libraries.

Very much was thought of writing ("penmanship"). As a rule, boys took delight in that. If a boy had gone through the Blue-back Speller, could write a clear legible hand, and had passed the "Rule of Three" in arithmetic, he was considered fairly well educated. Oh, yes, he must have given some time to the study of "Smith's English Grammar." Anyway, these things well and thoroughly learned were fundamental. Besides, there was much in the way of practical education that was learned on the farm and about the home.

The big time at the schoolhouse was on Friday afternoon, when the spelling match would come off and there was usually some attempt at public speaking. There had been no established standard of spelling until Noah Webster achieved it with his Blue-back Speller, which perhaps, accounts for the varied forms of spelling that prevailed. From that wonderful old spelling book came forth many champion spellers. The first pages contained the alphabet, followed by the elementary syllables. One had to learn his a-b abs. Progress was marked by certain stages. When one had reached "baker" and "shady" he was well into two syllables. There was the rule that every syllable in a word must be pronounced individually and as compounded, no matter how long the word nor if one of the component parts was only one letter. To spell the word *incomprehensibility,* the procedure would be, I-n in, c-o-m com, incom, p-r-e pre, incompre, h-e-n hen, incomprehen, s-i si, incomprehensi, b-i-l bil, incomprehensibil, i, incomprehensibili, t-y pronounced t-wy tie, accent on the wy, Incomprehensibility. To fail to spell and pronounce the word clearly and distinctly in this way was to miss. The spelling match was the main feature of the afternoon. All who were sufficiently advanced could take part without regard to age. This proved a strong incentive to all alike.

There was much rivalry in the speaking and much interest shown on the part of visitors. There were certain stock pieces that went the rounds as long as their popularity lasted. The first speaker would come out and declaim:

> "You would skyrce [scarce] expect
> One of my age
> To speak in public
> On the stage,
> And if I chance to fall below
> Demosthenes or Cicero,
> Don't view me with a cricket's [critic's) eye
> But pass my imperfections by."

It was a brave little boy who could deliver that. The next boy on the program essayed:

> "The boy stood on the burning deck
> whence all but him had fled."

Incidentally it may be remarked that the same boy stood on the deck many years on Friday afternoons. The story of "Mary Had A Little Lamb" was in the *height of* its popularity. These "pieces" were taken from *The Little Speaker,* but the teacher had a book for advanced students. It was a special favor to be permitted to make a selection from that. It contained such selections as, Mark Antony's Oration Over Caesar, Marmion's Defiance to Douglas, Supposed Speech of Lord Chatham on the American Revolution, Washington's Farewell Address, and sundry other patriotic American addresses, and a few other classics rather beyond the average boy in a rural school. If the teacher himself had the ability properly to train the boys they did creditably, otherwise there was much mutilation of material.

The larger girls depended for their recitations upon the minor English poets. "Maud Muller" and "Curfew Shall Not Ring Tonight" were not yet on the boards. "The Wreck of the Hesperus" was in sight, and "The Breaking Waves Dashed High."

## 15

## THE WAYFARER

The word tramp was not at that time included in the vocabulary of the backwoods, but there were frequently itinerant preachers, teachers, singing masters, bookkeepers, and "professors" of various sorts, who would come along and offer their services for whatever remuneration they could obtain. Some of those transients were worthwhile and happened along just when needed most.

There always have been human derelicts, and if backwoods records had been fully and accurately kept, it would be found that sometimes weary souls seeking to escape from a tragedy or great disappointment have found a haven of rest in some sequestered backwoods place among plain, kindly people—people a little shy of strangers and a little distrustful at first, but once their confidence was won were staunch in their friendship.

In the later times there came to Canoochee Backwoods whence, how or why, no one knew, a stranger, a man apparently about thirty-five years of age, shabby, unkempt, evidently ready to collapse from weariness and hunger. He was first seen at the store and post office. He was discovered by John Benton who had gone to the store on a shopping errand. Benton was a man of understanding and kindly sympathies. He soon saw that the man was not drunk but sick and starving and he took immediate charge of him. The man was assisted up from where he had fallen and placed in a big old armchair usually occupied by one of the idlers around the store. Restoratives were given, food in moderate quantity. It was found that the wayfarer should have a place to lie down. As he was not a fit object to introduce into one's clean home, a bed was improvised in a backroom of the store. There he slept until next morning, when soap, water and towel, followed by a hot breakfast from a nearby home wrought a considerable change in the man.

The stranger expressed appreciation for what had been done for him, and confessed that he was not really ill except from hunger and fatigue. Moreover, if they would permit him he would like to stay for a while and work for his board and a change of clothing.

To those who had befriended him, this stranger did not seem a common beggar, but as possessed of an innate dignity and sincerity. So they let him stay. He was given work and seemed ready and willing wherever needed. Tacitly, however, he was kept under surveillance for a time. Then it dawned upon some of them that this man was possessed of an intelligence and understanding far in advance of the average of the community. His dignified reserve and urbanity of manner won their respect.

The result was that if any one visiting in Canoochee Backwoods some years later had asked the name of the outstanding citizens, the first name given most probably would have been that of Judge Wilkins. So long had the wayfarer held a position of trust and honor in the community, no one seemed to know or remember anything about the manner of his coming among them, or to have heard the story of the man whom John Benton had found prone from hunger and fatigue on the porch of the country store.

And only to his warm personal friend, John Benton, had Raymond Wilkins revealed, and then in the briefest way, the story of his past life and the great tragedy—the story of a man's devotion and a woman's faithlessness, which had driven him forth, a wanderer from home and friends, into an almost unknown backwoods community. But there he had found peace and a partial surcease from haunting memories. There he had found friends, and he could mend the broken threads of his life in service to his fellow man.

## SUGAR CANE

Every farm in the lower South had its patch of sugar cane, and a very important crop it was, requiring only a small piece of land to produce syrup and sugar for the family the year round. The small farmer through this home product was independent of the extensive commercial output from the lowlands of Louisiana or elsewhere. The land had to be rich, but after the first planting very little cultivation was needed. At one time the farmers banked their seed cane when the stalks were cut for the syrup-making, and then in the spring opened up the great banks of earth, removed the stored cane and planted it.

Later it was found that a much better method and one that reduced the amount of work considerably and produced even better results, was to plant the cane at the time of cutting for the grinding. In this case the ground intended for the new crop of next year was plowed and made ready. The long trenches in which the seed stalks were to be laid received a heavy layer of pine or other straw and plentifully fertilizer. Then the stalks were carefully laid so as not to destroy the seed "eyes," a heavy covering of earth was drawn over the stalks, heavy enough to prevent any danger of frost, and they were left thus until the winter had passed and the warm days of spring had come. The earth covering, which had become somewhat depleted through the winter, was drawn away in part, so that the buried canes could receive the benefit of the warming sunshine and the rain. Later, the rows between the cane were plowed. It might be necessary to apply more fertilizer and plow again, but that would be all. The old roots from which the long ripe stalks had been cut were treated in a similar way to the seed stalks. There would be another crop from this stubble, but not quite so good as from the stalks.

When the stalks of ripe cane were cut, which was just before the danger of heavy frost, the immature green tops were cut off, the stalks stripped of their fodder and outer casing, and then carted to the mill and there heaped up ready for the grinding. The farmer's machinery for making syrup and sugar was of simple and primitive construction. The mill consisted of two heavy upright cylinders made to turn upon each other by means of corresponding cogs. The cylinders were placed upon a small but strong foundation. From the small screw propeller at the top of the frame a pole or sweep extended; to this was harnessed a slow-going horse or mule. Though the animal traveled slowly it was in a circle and a blindfold was necessary. As the mill was set going canes were thrust between the rollers; as the juice was crushed out it fell through a strainer of coarse cloth or sacking into a big cask.

An open shed housed the furnace which was built usually of clay, as that was the material most available, and the work could be done by members of the family. There were no scientific aids known to the backwoods then, and people had to depend upon practicable experience. However, there was always some man or perhaps a farmer woman whose experience and advice was invaluable when needed.

The juice was emptied into great shallow boilers or pans and a steady heat maintained beneath. Steady care and constant skimming were kept up in efforts at clarifying the boiling liquid. When the juice was sufficiently boiled it was poured into great troughs of seasoned hardwood that would not affect the flavor. The screened product was allowed to stand awhile, the syrup cool, and the sugar to solidify. The syrup was usually put into strong heavy casks. The sides of the syrup barrels were coated with crystal rock candy by the time the syrup was all used, which would be months later. Sugar was put into barrels with small holes bored in the bottom, the barrels then placed on a low, inclined platform arranged so that as the molasses dripped from the sugar it was caught in a receptacle beneath. To hasten the drainage of the molasses, stalks of the cane were thrust into the mass of sugar.

At one time the only uses to which the cane was put was the conversion into syrup and sugar, and the making of rum and vinegar. No account was taken of the refuse from the stalks as being of any value. But now the by-products are very valuable, two of these being a beautiful wall board, and cellophane. This last thin, clear and transparent as glass, tough and durable, makes a very attractive wrapping for any small merchandise. Score one more for science.

## SOWING AND REAPING

The annual work of the farm started early in the new year. There was the cleaning off and burning or plowing under of the refuse in the fields from last year's crop, like corn stalks and dead pea vines, such as had not been saved for forage. The only fences for the fields then were the worm fences made of rails split from the very plentiful supply of timber. The corners of these fences, both inside and outside, had to be cleaned out and the fences righted up. With the magnificent free ranges for cattle it was better to fence the crops rather than the cattle. With conditions somewhat reversed now, there are still sections in some parts of the South where the "no fence" law for crops is unpopular, and even hard to enforce, because public sentiment is against it. The backwoodsman holds to old customs, either from sentiment or from habit.

Corn was one of the earliest crops to be planted, cotton came later. Sweet potatoes were started early from a "draw bed." A small plot of ground was made into a rich soft bed of earth in which the sweet potatoes were planted very close without regard to anything except to get as many plants as could be made to sprout and grow from the bed. In the field where the potatoes were to grow, the land had been plowed and the earth drawn up into long high rows. The plants, or "draws," were then taken from the seed bed and set in the top of these long rows of earth. In a short time the plants would be growing finely, having been kept well watered if the season was unusually dry. Not only the tubers were growing in the soft earth, but long vines were growing at the top. These vines were clipped after a time and planted in the tops of similar rows of earth. And so on through the summer, vines were cut and planted in the potato rows, particularly after a summer rain. Potatoes from the "draws" matured early; those from the vines were left to grow until late fall.

From the first of April there was a succession of fresh vegetables, berries, melons and fruits. Watermelons of summer were grown in the fields and were intended only for home and neighborhood use, and not for market. Later the growing of watermelons for market has proven a profitable farming industry. Field peas were a forage crop, but then as now, when tender and green were considered fine for the table. Peas also were found to be of much value as a leguminous crop for soil improvement. At one time the maturing corn fodder was pulled from the stalks and used for forage. But that custom is being discarded now and other crops used along with the hay. When corn was matured there was the breaking of the corn from the stalks and letting it hang until the time came for harvesting.

Cotton required much care from the time it was planted. It had to be thinned, having been purposely planted too thick in order to get a good stand. Then came numerous hoeings "chopping"—and fertilizing until the cotton picking time. The farmer was fortunate who had sufficient help to tide over that time. It was better for the cotton not to hang onto the stalks in all sorts of weather. Perhaps the farmers by rotating with neighbors could get through. Cotton when picked was brought in from the field and each picker's share was recorded and a certain price paid to the outside helpers.

Later came the ginning. At one time the cotton seed was largely wasted, only a small part being saved for fertilizer. Then it was learned that the cotton seed was nearly as valuable as the cotton itself. Volumes could be, and may have been, written upon the subject of cotton seed and the multitude of products that are being manufactured from it, many of them valuable food products and known nearly all over the world.

## 16

### GARDENING

The vegetable garden was a very important source of food supply. At the ending of the old year and the beginning of the New Year, before the farm work had started, and when the men and boys had leisure to help, the garden was gone over. If the family had kept the same garden spot for a long time, it might be thought best to move the garden, or take in new ground. Land was so plentiful and cheap this sort of rotation of crops was commendable and more satisfactory than an intensive tilling of the same plot. Very early in the year the more hardy vegetables, English peas and Irish potatoes, when these last were not intended for the public market, could be planted. After the 10th of March in the lower Southern latitudes even tender vegetables could be set. Before that time the lettuce and young onions were sufficiently grown for salad, while the sprouts from the stalks of collards which had been allowed to stand after the heads had been cut, made very appetizing "greens." There were no canned fruits and vegetables at that time. Tomatoes were not considered edible and were not planted in the vegetable garden, although the plants were sometimes found in the flower yard, where they were known by the fanciful name of "love apples." The fruit was small and in no way could compare with the fine product of the later highly cultivated varieties.

Along in April new Irish potatoes and English peas were plentiful. This was the time when young spring chickens were coming in as broilers. With roses blooming in the front yard—in that section roses did not wait until June to shower forth their bloom—with bees humming all around the hives, hens and chickens clucking and cheeping about the place; fruit trees shedding their blooms; sweetness in the air, it was time to go fishin'.

Cantaloupes were planted in the garden, watermelons in the field. Was there ever anything more delicious than a ripe Southern watermelon? They did not ripen, however, until the hot weather. Green corn came in May, also dewberries and plums of the smaller variety, other fruits later on in the season. The vegetable garden contained a greater or less variety of herbs; many for medicinal value, others perhaps for their fragrance. As the red pepper ripened it was strung in strands and hung up to dry for winter use. Sage, so fine for seasoning sausage and other winter meat was dried and powdered, closely covered and set away. The dried pepper was ground; mustard seed was ground or macerated in a small iron mortar, screened and dried. Other herbs were dried and cared for in similar ways, ready for use.

Truck gardening on a large scale was not carried on except in the neighborhood of cities and large towns. Transportation facilities were not then adequate for perishable stuff. There were no refrigerator cars; all the ice used in the warm latitudes of the South was shipped from the North, and little if any ever reached the remote backwoods sections. It was in 1858 that the formula for the production of artificial ice was released by Dr. John B. Gorrie, and its general use was not known until after the Civil War. Besides, it was after that period that the advantages of diversified farming were realized in the lower South. When the era of the automobile and the building of good roads set in there was a wonderful revolution in the lives and occupations of the people everywhere.

## FOOD CONSERVATION

Within the past several decades science has done much for improvement in methods of food conservation, particularly as applied to the domestic output. In those old days nothing was known to any housewife about the preservation of fruits and vegetables by sterilization and the hermetically sealing of jars and cans. Steam pressure cookers in the home had never been heard of, or even thought of, perhaps, except by men making scientific research.

Meats were dried, smoked or pickled. It was found that sausage put in a stone jar and completely covered by melted lard and allowed to stand would keep indefinitely. Fruits were preserved in sugar; or those that lent themselves to the method were dried by a primitive process of placing in the sun; and success depended upon the state of the weather during the period of drying. Even then there was the trouble of keeping the fruit screened from insects. Some vegetables also were dried in a similar way, or pickled. Beans and peas naturally dried on the stalks and vines, but these had to be looked after that no weevils spoiled them. The bulk of the peas and beans was kept in the big barn, but what was intended for family use was put in cloth sacks and hung in the store room to one of the joists along with the garden seeds for the next planting. The first commercially dried vegetables were called "desiccated" and had to be soaked in water before cooking-like beans.

All these operations called for much work which would have been reduced to a minimum if there had been any certainty that after preparation everything would keep, but climatic conditions and methods largely determined the question. Now, when a housewife packs a can of tomatoes or other vegetable or fruit, she knows that if she has used proper care the contents of cans and jars are safe for an indefinite time, and there will be no loss or disappointment thereby.

Honey was stored both in the comb and strained, the latter method being the better, perhaps. Besides the domestic honey from bees on the home place, there was often wild honey to be found by the bee hunter.

There were many nuts to be gathered from the woods in the fall of the year—chinquapins (a sort of chestnut), hickory nuts, walnuts, and these, with the home-grown peanuts (commonly known as "pinders"), made cracking nuts a pleasant diversion around the winter fireside. In the spring and early summer, dewberries, blackberries, huckleberries (nobody outside the dictionary ever called them "whortle" berries), May pops—the fruit of the passion flower—haws, and crab apples (good for preserving) made a pleasant round of wild fruits. A most delicious fruit found in old fields in the fall of the year was the wild persimmon. Persimmons were the main ingredient of a very excellent homemade beer, which was usually flavored with sassafras root, and was very similar in taste to a much advertised popular drink of today.

Some hardy vegetables could be grown throughout the winter. In the late summer and early fall large "patches" of turnips, both the white kind and the yellow rutabagas were sown, also collards, a variety of cabbage. These at their best furnished "greens" for the family table and were good for cows and chickens.

Sweet potatoes were highly regarded as an article of food, and were found on the family table every day for months. They admitted many ways of serving, baked, boiled, fried, candied, and in custard pie which was a rich combination with milk, sugar, butter, eggs and flavoring. Sweet potato pone was made from grated raw potatoes, mixed with cane syrup, some sugar, a large lump of good sweet lard, various spices, and the whole mass made quite soft with plenty of rich sweet milk, and slowly baked, being frequently turned from the sides of the oven as it browned. The oven for baking was an iron Dutch oven like that in which lightbread was baked. It was set on the kitchen hearth and fire placed both on top and underneath the oven. This was regular potato "pone" and when cold was cut in slices to serve. The spices made it quite dark, which was considered just the right thing.

To make sweet potato pudding was to select only the lightest colored yams and omit the spices that would turn it dark and substitute orange peel or lemon peel, use white sugar, but no syrup; make the mass very soft with rich sweet milk, pour into the oven and bake. The method of baking was nearly the same as for the pone, stirring frequently and turning from sides as the crust formed. Baking was a long slow process; the result a richly browned pudding with an amber-colored interior that was goodness itself, and soft enough to serve with a spoon. Golden brown cornbread was an indispensable article of food found on the table in regular succession every day.

Many articles of daily food consumption which now come ready for use in cans, jars and cartons, then had to be prepared almost entirely in the home kitchen. Spices were ground in a small mill usually fastened on the kitchen wall, or they were macerated in a small, heavy iron mortar similar to the mortar used by the druggist in compounding prescriptions. Allspice and black pepper were ground, ginger and nutmegs were grated with a small grater. Mace, and cinnamon which comes in thin dried bark, were pounded in the iron mortar. The small mill was sometimes used for dried red pepper from the home garden. The method of cleaning the spice mill for its varied uses was to run some dry grits or meal through it several times.

This method thoroughly cleaned the mill and left no trace from one to the other of the spices ground in it.

Coffee was roasted and ground at home. The favorite kind of green coffee was Rio, a pure South American product. Another green coffee was the peaberry, so-called from the shape of the grain which resembled a garden pea. Coffee was cheap in those days. The finer grades like Java and Mocha were much higher, but the Rio produced a clear strong beverage which was much liked.

The method of preparing the raw coffee was to look it over by hand, rejecting any stray gravel or other refuse, wash and dry the coffee and roast it in a big iron "spider" on the kitchen hearth with a moderate fire underneath, constantly stirring to prevent scorching. The stirring was sometimes done with a longhandled spoon, but there was in nearly every kitchen a long slender paddle of oak or hickory which was reserved for stirring the roasting coffee. Just before the coffee had reached the full degree of roasting and browning, and was nearly ready to be removed from the spider, a small piece of pure sweet butter or a very small piece of pure lard was added to the coffee and stirred all through it. This glaze tends to make the coffee settle when prepared for drinking. When the coffee was taken from the fire and was somewhat cooled it was put into a tightly closed receptacle to prevent the escape of aroma and strength. When the coffee was to be brewed, the dry roasted grains were ground in the mill, measured and put into the metal coffee pot with cold water and brought to a boil on the coals; or boiling water was poured upon the dry ground coffee in the pot and barely permitted to continue the boiling, when it was ready to be poured off into the cups—a most delicious beverage it proved to be.

At a later time there appeared for sale in the cities and larger towns new designs in coffee pots bearing more or less claim to their merits in producing the best coffee; but those improved coffee pots did not at once find their way to the backwoods. Meanwhile the old-time backwoods housekeepers rather prided themselves upon the quality, and quantity as well, of the coffee they offered others and drank themselves. The sound and odor of fresh coffee being ground was most welcome, particularly in the early morning when it was an unfailing signal for breakfast. The odor of coffee accompanied by that of fine home-cured bacon, or ham, with fresh eggs made an appeal to any healthy, red-blooded individual, whether in the backwoods or anywhere else.

## POULTRY

On every farm some poultry was raised. Where the farm women gave intelligent care to their flocks the work was found both interesting and profitable. They had all the advantages of food in abundance at little or no extra cost; wide range and space, with sunlight and shade, fresh air and water. The children of the family were generally glad to help with the work. The nearness of a creek or a pond made the keeping of geese and ducks much easier. The mothers of young turkeys had to be watched to keep them from running out into the grass and dew of the early morning. Young turkeys do not thrive under such treatment, and it is fatal to young goslings to get caught in a shower. Geese were kept for their feathers. The traditional household wedding gift from a mother was a big feather bed and pillows; and the feathers and down that went into the making had to be from the live geese raised on the home place.

There were many enemies to the poultry flocks, which had to be taken into account and various defenses raised against them. Skunks, 'possums and hawks were the worst. Guinea fowls were often kept as a sentinel against hawks. Their incessant call of "Pot Rack! Pot Rack!" was a cheerful note and a signal when needed to give notice of the nearness of a hawk. There were always guns high up on the walls of the hall, and a light shotgun that a boy or his mother could use against a hawk. Most of the farm women could shoot.

A noisy welcome met the approach of a stranger to a backwoods farmhouse. The horses neighed and whinnied; hound dogs bayed; the other dogs barked; geese screamed; ducks quacked; guinea fowls called "Pot Rack!"; and the big rooster, the patriarch of his family, set up a loud crow. Sometimes the timid little children not used to strangers, hid and fearfully peeped from their hiding places; women withdrew. At the stranger's loud salutation of "Halloa!" "Halloa!" the man of the house if anywhere in front called back, "light! light! [Alight] and come in," and went to ward off the dogs. Then it was "Howdye, Howdye" from each of them, and much vigorous handshaking.

## 17

## CATTLE

One custom that prevailed then but greatly condemned now was the burning of the woods in late winter to hasten the growth of young grass for the cattle in the early spring. It was not so harmful to burn the woods then. With a great expanse of woods with the big standing timber that would not be needed for many years to come, the rank undergrowth and heavy native grass, the destruction of the undergrowth did not mean so much then. Within the past seventy or more years there has been a wanton waste of the magnificent timber in consequence of which there is urgent need, not only for conservation, but also for the stupendous system of reforestation recently inaugurated.

When there was a plentiful growth of young grass on the "burn" the cattle were brought home from the range, the deep woods and canebrakes. The spring roundup of the cattle would take several days, dependent largely upon the inclination of the cattle about leaving their swampy vastnesses, and whether they were easy to drive. This was a business in which the men and boys liked to engage. The cracking of the long whips could be heard a long way off, and with the "cow holla," which the cattle seemed to understand and like, it was thrilling. As they approached the home, the men and boys on horseback accompanied by the faithful dogs, all the family came out to see. "There they come! Oh, see the calves!" were glad exclamations at sight of the moving herd.

The big cowpens had been made ready and the cattle were driven in. If there were too many cattle for the pens they were first driven into a field. Then came the counting and dividing off. The dry cattle were turned back on the range, while the mothers and young calves were kept. There was always a large number of young calves.

Some of them had come as early as January, so by the time they were brought home the cows were ready to yield a part of their milk for the family—but only a part, as it was important that the calves have plenty of milk and be not stunted in their growth. The cows were milked in the open cowpens. While the milking was going on the calves had to be "minded off" so that they would not get more than their share. This duty fell to the children of the family, who felt duly rewarded by being permitted to claim as their own any cow and calf in the bunch that they saw fit. If the father acted in good faith with the children (and many of them did), the increase from the gift went to the child and laid the foundation of his future prosperity. Besides, the children were thus taught lessons in stock raising, and given an inspiration to work.

The cows were kept in the cowpen at night and turned out on the grass in the daytime. This order was reversed with the calves, which were kept in a little pasture of their own in the daytime and were not with their mothers except at milking time. The older cattle were already marked and branded, and the marking and branding of the calves was done just before the milk cows were turned back upon the range, about the first week in August. Throughout the winter the cattlemen looked after the stock and kept account of them. If a cow did not get enough to eat she became weak and might fall into a ditch or bog. In that case she would be propped up and fed until strong enough to be brought home for further attention. A calf one year old was a "yearling" and one two years old a "herdic," often called a "harrydick." Nobody then and there had ever heard of a "maverick."

Oxen were useful on a place for heavy hauling of logs and timber or lumber where slow steady movement was wanted. Most farmers had one or two pairs that were turned out on the range with the other cattle when not needed. They were not expensive to keep. The oxen at work needed plenty of corn and hay and good regular care; they could get their own living when on the range. When a farmer needed to break in a new pair of oxen there were plenty of men and boys who liked to take part as spectators at least; but the real work had to be done by men who knew their business, and were cool, level-headed and alert. Strong, healthy young steers were selected; these were driven into the horse lot or barnyard, one with a high fence was all the better. It might have to be resorted to as a place of safety before the business was over.

The first step was to lasso the steer with a good strong rope of the proper size to hold it without being clumsy. Precaution had been taken that the animal should not be unduly excited in the beginning, but when he felt the rope around his horns, he did become excited and protest his treatment by very vigorous action—bowing and violently shaking his head, roaring, bellowing, pawing the earth, and plunging wildly about. Noting the fire in his eye and the sharpness of his horns, it seemed best to keep out of his way. But the rope was held by strong determined hands. The animal was allowed to tire himself out without receiving any bodily injury. That was the purpose—to let the creature know that there was a force too strong for him to buck against.

Having subdued the animal to the degree where he could no longer resist, the next step was to complete the conquest by kindness. Shortening the length of rope, the men would approach the steer and rub him gently on the back and about the head and face until the animal began to understand that his captors meant to be kind. Talking in gentle tones and the stroking were kept up until the response seemed complete. When it was found that the confidence of the animal was completely gained, it was easy enough for the men to proceed. Another steer, apparently equal in every way, selected to be the running mate was secured in similar fashion. Then the two had the yoke placed across their strong necks and secured by the bows fashioned on each. The big gate of the barn-lot was now opened, and the two men, one on each side, lengthening, but still holding to the ropes, the animals were brought out. A heavy drag, either a log, or a ladder-like construction prepared for the purpose, was attached and the pair of oxen were taught to pull and draw. Much kindly and encouraging talk was kept up during the trial. If the oxen were intended for plowing, which was the case in the earlier days, instead of the yoke the steer would have a pair of hames and a collar around his neck attached to trace chains for his lesson in pulling and drawing. Plowing oxen had to get used to the rattling of the trace chains as well as learn to pull and draw. The plow was introduced later.

As the training progressed, the animals showed much docility and intelligence. With a rope on each pair of horns and a man on each side they were guided along. One man supplied with a heavy-handled braided whip with a buckskin cracker on the end, enforced commands with a crack of the whip. The animals soon learned to follow the sound of the whip, that "Gee" meant *right*, and that "Haw" meant *left*, and "Whoa" was *stop*. Failure to stop brought a flick on the nose that was not disregarded. The load was increased from time to time until a reasonable limit was reached. Then came the attaching of the oxen to the big timber cart with its heavy load of logs or timber—though this trial was delayed perhaps until the next day, and the animals rested until then.

When the timber to be hauled was very heavy, more than one pair of oxen was needed. Oxen were better adapted for hauling through the woods than mules, particularly where logs had to be brought from swampy places. The woods were the natural habitat of the oxen, and they could be relied upon to do the work where mules would bog. Mules were all right in the smooth woods or on roads. Horses were not at all fitted for the hauling of logs from the woods, not even the big draft horses. The size and shape of the feet and hoofs of draft animals has to be taken into account. The ox was the first domesticated beast of burden of civilization.

*These sketches, which began in the issue for March 1938, relate largely to Bryan County, Georgia, through which the Canoochee River flows. Their time is around the third quarter of the Nineteenth Century. They are based mainly on the reminiscences of Miss Harn, who is now well beyond four score years. Editor

*18*

## HOUSES

Development of the sawmill industry and the manufacture of lumber became a business of gigantic proportions in the backwoods at a later time, but in those earlier days the people were greatly handicapped by the lack of ready building material. Sawmills and manufacturing plants were scarce and far away, and transportation facilities inadequate. Most of the houses in Canoochee Backwoods were built of logs; chimneys generally of clay and sticks, instead of brick. All the farms were fenced with homesplit rails and formed in the "worm fence" pattern, which proved very satisfactory for the fields in every way, and besides, the rails lasted a long time. For the front yard fence where pickets were not available, long strips riven by hand were nailed to upright posts.

Garden "palings" were very necessary to bar out rabbits and other marauding animals. Chickens also had to be protected. Some families let the grown fowls rest in treetops. Where this was done there was an obstruction nailed around the body of the tree to keep away skunks (polecats), Billy 'possum or any other animal with a taste for stolen chicken. For the garden palings, which had to be six feet or more in height, long blocks were riven with the maul and wedge and finished by hand into long boards like shingles. The garden posts were generally "lightwood" posts found about woods and fields, or perhaps were cedar. Strips were nailed at intervals between the posts, and the long paling boards "wattled" in and out close together so as to leave no cracks between for the rabbits to get through. The tops of those palings having been sharply pointed before building them into the fence, the vegetables growing in the garden were well protected. Some shingles, usually of pine, were also riven by hand from the blocks.

The young pine trees growing so tall and straight and beautiful in the woods furnished logs for the houses. Pines were especially adapted because they grew so tall without projecting branches through much of their length, and were of nearly uniform diameter for several feet. A log house built with proper regard for its requirements and with a neat and symmetrical finish is both attractive in appearance and very comfortable. The manner of building the chimneys was to form the chimney proper throughout of sticks fashioned for the purpose, then daub the structure inside and out with clay. The heart was built up from the ground. With a wide hearth and a fireplace of proper height in front and a neat mantel above, the chimney was an attractive as well as a desirable feature of the house. In those country homes there were great glowing fires in winter, which made a delightful resort for the family. In summer the fireplaces was kept filled with green boughs from the woods.

The house rested upon heavy pine blocks set well off the ground. There were many reasons why this was desirable. Where possible, manufactured lumber from the nearest sawmill was brought for floors, windows and many of the finishings for the house, although there were not always glass window panes in the windows.

An enterprising man among the citizens would sometimes set up a turning lathe down by the millsite for the manufacture of wooden ware of many kinds—churns, water pails, and barrels. With the aid of his turning lathe he could manufacture earthen ware jugs, jars and bowls. The blacksmith and wheelwright shop were indispensable in every backwoods neighborhood. There was a time when every part of the wagons and other vehicles had to be made completely by hand with the turning lathe and whatever iron tools could be secured.

When a new house was to be built, the trees were selected from the forest, felled, cut into proper lengths and the pine bark removed. All this having been made ready, invitations to the house raising were sent out to the neighbors. Nearly every man able to contribute anything would respond. Bright and early the work started. With so many strong men working and with the knowledge of just what to do, they would get results in an incredibly short time.

The women of the neighborhood also took a part in the work. Certain of them would come the day before and assist the other housewife with the cooking, for it goes without saying that a large amount of food would be required. Perhaps some woman neighbor would make a contribution of cooked food from her own home. This was all done in friendly fashion. Kindness and good will prevailed.

It was planned that the work would not consume the entire day, and there would be a good social time all around—a great hearty dinner, jollity and feasting intermingled. The affair would end up with a party that night. To see those fine, healthy young swains in the dance and the folk plays, with all the pretty girls of the neighborhood, was a delight. They had worked hard nearly all day, but who would guess it then?

The similar gathering to that of the house raising would be the log rolling. "You help me, and I'll help you," was the idea. Is the politician's idea of "log rolling" the same? If a farmer wanted to clear an old field of standing timber, or take in an extra piece of land, the neighbors came, the trees were felled, and with long pikes, several men at each log, would roll and pile the logs into hug heaps and set fire to them while there, or else the farmer would burn the logs himself. No such waste of timber is practiced now. Trees may be felled, the stumps removed with a stump pulling machine or else they are blown out with dynamite, but in each case the timber is salvaged.

The backwoods house raising or the log rolling was always followed by a neighborhood party that night. In those days women made a great many patchwork quilts, some of which were really beautiful. When the time came to quilt the patchwork into a finished product, women and girls from the neighborhood would come and do the work. And a great time it was for jollity and frolicking for the young people. Sometimes there would be young men there ahead of the expected time who came under the pretext of threading needles for the girls. All this irregularity led to more fun. Happy, Happy Days!

# 19

## OUTDOOR SPORTS

With the fine outdoor life led by the people of Canoochee Backwoods there was little need for formal athletics. There was no standardized baseball; English football was not played then in America, and when introduced was absorbed by the big colleges. The young men played ball after a fashion of their own. They had games of running, leaping, jumping, pole vaulting, whipcracking contests; and any worthwhile boy could "skin the cat" on the horizontal bar. All the men, boys, women and girls, rode horseback. The youngsters learned to ride when they sat before their father on horseback and later on when they were seated alone and held, to keep from falling off. Impromptu horse racing was common enough, but there was no regular racing for stakes. When the boys were scarcely more than babies they were taken to the creek and plunged in, so that later they became accomplished swimmers.

The woods was full of game of many kinds. Though there was little if any restrictions, the hunting season was well defined and certain ethical rules prevailed to govern the conduct of the hunters. Every family kept some hounds. Dogs were useful not only for hunting, but were a great help with the cattle; they were intelligent and loyal in their friendship for the family. Every stock raiser spent much time on the cattle range, and he rarely appeared anywhere from home without his faithful hounds. In addition to the hounds, there were nearly always other dogs on the place, usually an ordinary cur for small services about the home, and to accompany the boys in their night sports in coon and 'possum hunting. In return for their services the dogs needed food and care; this they received in generous degree. The women of the family might complain about the quantity of cooked food required in addition to the raw meat, but the men and the children demanded lavish portions for their favorites. After all, it was the children and dogs who gave the charm to the country home, and made the life there worth living.

## BARBECUES

The art of storytelling had been inherited from their British forebears, and the boys and girls profited by the tales, classic and otherwise, that had been handed down to them. They had all heard about George Washington and the cherry tree. They knew about the "Fo'th" of July, which was annually celebrated by a fish fry on the river bank. Great loads of the finest watermelons and hampers of food with the fish, made the day one of feasting and jollity. For frying the fish, somebody brought along the big iron washpot which had been scoured and made ready. The fish, caught in advance and dressed, were plunged into the gallons of boiling fat in the pot, and when sufficiently browned were taken out and drained. This duty was performed by two men who were expert outdoor cooks and took much interest in the work.

Sometimes as a change from the fish fry, there would be a barbecue. This required expert cookery, indeed, and the man who possessed the artistic skill and executive ability to conduct successfully the barbecue for a big political gathering was held in high esteem. It should be remembered that the voters in the Backwoods were not neglected by the candidates in a campaign year, and that the barbecue was the popular form of outdoor feasting for a political rally. The master of the feast was found and his services secured in advance. For the cooking, a wide pit or trench several feet in length was dug in a selected piece of ground, and was so arranged as to permit the burning of great quantities of hardwood to a huge bed of glowing coals, on which the beef and pork were roasted and broiled. This meat, just at the right time, was carved and served to the crowd, along with whatever other food was available. Everybody seemed in good humor. There was much spread eagle oratory by the candidates; and jokes and compliments followed as the order of the day. Whatever of triumphs or disappointments may have come to the candidates from the rally, the friendly outdoor gathering of the people of the neighborhood did much to emphasize a kindly spirit among them.

## GOIN' TO TOWN

Of all the enjoyable happenings, the best was Goin' to Town. The larger boys always went; girls and smaller boys took turn about. The mother rarely went, and not at any time when there was a baby—and there was always a baby in the period when the mother was young enough to enjoy the trip and its attendant features. But she enjoyed the event in a vicarious way, and lent her aid to those who did go, in getting them ready the lunch for the first day of the journey, which took the better part of two days, with their slow mode of traveling and the fact that they stopped to spend the first night on the way with relatives and friends.

The time selected for the trip for the younger members of the family was in the early fall, and sometimes in the early spring. The father may have had to go on business at other times, and, if the business did not take too long, he could easily make the trip and back in one day, nearly always reaching home in the early night. But as the juniors wanted to get all they could out of the visit, they were permitted to make the over-night stop.

In the early fall after the cotton picking was over and the cotton had been ginned, baled, and shipped to Savannah, the father must go to manipulate the sale. He knew pretty well in advance what he was to receive, since he had had offers from the firm who had been his factors for years. There was a sort of mutual pledge between them. The factor, as the name indicates, transacted all the business for the farmer in town, lent him money when he needed it, and performed any service of an unusual character for the farmer or his family. In return, the factor had the first choice in the purchase of the farmer's cotton at a fair market price, and deducted reasonable commission for such services he had rendered that were worthwhile paying for. In this way a strong business friendship was established that was mutually pleasant.

The early fall was selected for the visit of the boys and girls for the reason that while the hay had been saved and the cotton was in the market, there were other crops yet to be harvested a little later on. The corn was still hanging to the stalks, the sweet potatoes would be to dig and bank; and then the one big joyful time of hard work and fun was to come later in the cane-grinding. That would be not long over when the hog-killing time would come, a little in advance of the Christmas holidays, the season of parties. So, looking ahead and counting all those things which make a pleasant round of activities on the farm, this seemed the best time for goin' to town.

The father would sell the cotton, as that was the money crop, and the youngsters would get a share of the proceeds. The father was always liberal enough when it came down to the very last, but he never parted with any money to the children until he had paid all the debts—and there were bound to be some debts. Then was the time to buy the quarterly supply of "store" goods-the barrel of flour, coffee, and so on, besides a few things for the kitchen which mother greatly needed. The farm tools were usually bought in the spring, but there might be now an absolute need for a new saddle or bridle, or a set of harness—and these must be considered first.

After these necessary things were purchased, the boys and girls would go with father to buy the family shoes—a pair of tiny red shoes for the baby girl at home, a pair for mother, and some pairs for the other children, all of whose measurements one of the girls had brought along. Also, she had the memorandum of the other articles needed or wanted. Was ever a farm woman to go to town without that precious memorandum? Surely not, in those days or since.

The older girls wanted to go to the camp meeting at Taylors Creek in Liberty county, that was to come off later. There must be shoes and hats and dresses for that occasion and "a few" other things so dear to the feminine heart. Well, they did get nearly what they wanted. They went home all as happy as larks, and would not have swapped their father for any other father in the whole world, besides having the best mother in the country waiting for them at home. Along with all this the boys had found just the best place to sell their pigs they were fattening at home; and the turkeys the girls would have to sell at Thanksgiving and Christmas. The boys kept the money their father had given them for some extra work on the farm; this they would keep and add to their pig money later on, so that after awhile they would have something worthwhile to invest.

# THE ALL-DAY SING

The All-Day Sing was scheduled to come off at Hickory Branch Church next Sunday. Since no "worldlian" songs would be sung, the singing would take the place of the regular worship. For weeks past classes had been preparing for the contest. These were mostly girls and young men from the singing school which met every two weeks. But the contest had been declared open to any others who wished to enter. This blanket announcement had been regretted when it was learned that Sister Sary-Ann Davis had joined one of the classes, and was going to try for the honor and the prize to be given to the best singer among the women. There was another prize for the men.

It was well known that Sister Sary-Ann Davis could not sing true to key, no matter what she thought about it. Indeed, she was one of those unfortunate individuals who become obsessed with an exaggerated idea of their own talents to the detriment of anything of a social or public nature in which they see fit to engage. Sister Sary-Ann not only could not sing true to key, but she so annoyed and put out others that they could not sing. What was to be done about it?

The contest was to be conducted by classes. There were to be some individual singers-soloists, besides a duet and a quartet from each class, and the class chorus. All of the disgruntled ones were willing to let Sister Sary-Ann Davis try her voice as a soloist, but she wanted to sing "high trible" in a quartet from one of the classes. And she did, when the time came.

As early as eight o'clock on the appointed Sunday people began to arrive at the church. Many families came in open farm wagons with chairs for women and girls; the boys sitting as best they could without the chairs. There were a carryall or two—The Blantons and Captain Edward's family had such a turnout. Several open buggies, and a few top buggies, all pretty well filled, were unloaded. Nearly always there was an engaged couple who were objects of attention, which they seemed to enjoy. A number of girls and young men rode horseback. The farmer girls were nearly as fine riders as their brothers, being hampered only by the prescribed custom of riding sideways. No woman rode astride then; neither in the towns where horseback riding was a popular pastime, nor in the countryside. For a girl to be seen riding in that fashion would have been to put her beyond the pale.

Among the earliest arrivals were several equestrian couples. Each man had rivaled the other in securing for his companion the best rider among the girls in the neighborhood, and to come down to modern form of speech, had made a date in advance, probably weeks ahead.

Before every farmhouse front gate, in addition to the hitching posts where one could checkrein a horse, was a pair of heavy wooden blocks, side by side, one a little higher than the other, and known as a horse block. This was for the convenience of the women in mounting and dismounting. But there was no such manner of mounting and dismounting when a gentleman was along. The girl simply placed one foot in the gentleman's hand and was instantly and gracefully seated upon her horse. This was a gallant gesture which each young cavalier took much pride in being able to perform in a manner that conferred distinction upon both the girl and himself.

Just here it is well to note the changes that have taken place in equestrian styles between that day and this. The use of sidesaddles for women was not completely discarded until about 1900, although there had been indications of their disuse earlier than that. Probably there are none to be seen now outside of museums. The stylish equestrienne outfit for a society lady of that time was elaborate and would excite comment now.

A lady's fine side-saddle with its accompanying trappings of saddle cloth, bridle and quirt was lightly expensive. The saddle was made of the finest leather, large, roomy-seated. It had two pommels, horn-like projections, often called horns, between which the rider's right knee was to rest when she assumed the sidewise position. The saddle cloth, made of very fine wool with corners embossed or decorated in some way, was placed on the horse's back; upon this the saddle was securely strapped by a strong leather girth. The handsome bridle having been adjusted, the outfit was ready. What were known as martingales were useless ornamental appendages to the bridle, which were caught by a strap that was passed under the horse's chest and fastened to the saddle girth.

With this outfit the lady wore a riding habit of a soft and beautiful wool fabric; a very full and long skirt, coming well below her feet when seated; above this a short jacket and a small hat with a long plume or scarf; with the usual riding gloves and quirt. It speaks well for the women riders that they were able to sit so erect and not get a fatal fall.

The riding habit of the farmer girl was much simpler, and consisted of a very full skirt, usually of homespun, open on one side and buttoned securely around the waist. The skirt was sufficiently long to cover the rider's dress, and being of thick material, afforded protection against dust. As she usually rode a man's saddle, which was smaller, the farmer girl had more freedom of movement and was safer. Moreover, with a change of gloves, the rustic beauty was quite fresh and becomingly dressed when her riding habit had been laid aside, and ready to enter anywhere, whereas, the lady with the handsome riding habit must carry her long skirt on her left arm when dismounted. Sometimes a married woman rode "double" with her husband, but girls did not ride that way unless running away to be married.

But all this is a digression, while they are gathering at the church—and they brought the children. Did ever any one see so many babies at church? It looked as if they would have a few solos, and even choruses, not down on the program. The Backwoods people believed in taking their babies to church. For one reason, it was considered the bounden duty of every mother to take care of her child and be burdened with it when anyone else rejected the responsibility. So, no matter where she went, the mother had to take the baby along, or stay at home.

In some communities of primitive people it was permissible to lay a pallet of quilts down just under the pulpit where the baby or babies, since there might be more than one, could sleep, or kick up their little pink heels in perfect abandon. It was not strange that in those communities the preacher rather encouraged the bringing of the little children to the long services. He liked to have a large congregation, and if the little children were there it insured the presence of other members of the family. The preacher advised that it was well to establish very early the habit of church-going, to "bring up a child in the way he should go."

By half-past eight the congregation was seated in the large church. The services were opened with a scriptural reading and prayer. Classes were formed; a committee was named who retired to the outdoors to nominate the judges and elected by ballot. These preliminaries being disposed of, the judges took their seats. They were three men and two women, elderly individuals, who had led the singing in former times and were supposed to be skilled in church music. The action of the nominating committee was probably known in advance since the election of the judges was unanimous. Deacon Jones who had been made chairman of the program now announced the contest open and called the classes in the order named.

The first class to respond had as a leader Brother George William Watkins. There was no musical instrument, only a triangle. The first hymn was announced. All the singers had large music books with shaped notes, "The Sacred Harp." The books were opened, the scale was sung. Brother Watkins with the aid of the triangle pitched the key. The first hymn was rendered with clear young voices and fairly well. Then came one that made everybody sit up and listen. This was something that had been talked of in advance, and all were expecting a surprise. It was Sister Caroline Watkins who sponsored the innovation. Sister Watkins was a very ambitious woman, and was accused of always trying to introduce newfangled ways into the life of the community, of which the more staid and conservative did not approve. She had a cousin living in Savannah with whom Sister Watkins sometimes exchanged visits. This cousin was a "fashionable woman," whose airs and graces were a source of much irritation, if not a positive offense to the good women of Canoochee Backwoods who met her on her occasional visits.

Sister Watkins had not long returned from a visit to that same cousin in Savannah and while there had attended church where they had a trained choir. Sister Watkins was not much of a singer herself, but she greatly enjoyed the anthem in the city church. She tried to describe to her husband, who could sing by note, just how a part-time piece of music had been rendered, and persuaded him to attempt a similar performance with his class in the contest. Brother Watkins was doubtful of his ability, the more particularly as he had not heard the music, and had to depend for his understanding upon his wife's description; but he tried to please her in the matter. He did not have the material found in a trained church choir, but Brother Watkins in his bungling way did his best, and failed. However, Sister

Watkins got the blame from the listeners. The desire of the woman was right, perhaps, she was just the victim of her own ignorance and misinterpretation of what she had heard in the city church. Although the judges did not understand, they decided among themselves that the performance was only another of Sister Watkins' efforts to introduce unwonted innovations into the affairs of the community, and were kind enough to pass the matter by without comment.

A leader of one of the classes was a dapper little man with a great accession of dignity. At a former time he had kept school in the backwoods for two terms, and had ever since then been known as "Professor" Elber Matthews, a distinction he seemed greatly to enjoy. He moved quickly, but at the same time was so painfully precise in his manner, that he crushed all spontaneity out of his class, so there were now only two men under his leadership. One young woman, stout, robust and daring, assumed an air of boldness and literally roared, looking at him as with disdain at his efforts to mark time.

The next to follow was the opposite of the last leader. He had a lively manner, seeming to discard dignity and to discover something very pleasant if not highly amusing in his position. His self-complacency was so evident he must have expected to win. He marked time in a most active manner, moving his arms up, down, and aside. These movements coupled with the fact his shoulders were much humped, and the funny little coat he wore was much too short-waisted in the back, gave him a ludicrous appearance when viewed from the rear.

There had been short intervals between classes and now dinner was announced. Baskets were opened and for convenience of everybody the viands were spread on the rough plank tables under the big trees in the rear of the church; and great jugs of cool water were brought from the spring just under the hill. The Canoochee housewives sustained their reputation in the matter of the dinner. The older of the small boys and girls had cared for the little children in the cool outdoors, and watched over the babies while they slept. The tired mother appreciated the rest. Dinner and friendly conversation made a pleasant episode of the day. They returned to the church and the singing was resumed.

In one of the classes was a solemn, elderly man, who sang in a way peculiarly his own. His strong nasal intonation was employed at intervals at the end of a line with a sound something like this—Mhmmhm. To one listening, it seemed that the man was registering his satisfaction at his own performance.

Now came what many were looking forward to with much interest. There had been group singing, solos, duets, which though not specially remarkable, had passed muster. The looked-for quartet included two men, tenor and bass, a woman alto, and Sister Sary-Ann Davis as "high trible." It was a hard trial for the two men and the other woman who could sing. Sister Sary-Ann's treble was pretty high in the first stanza; she seemed to gain strength and height in the second; and in the third and last to score her final triumph; which was registered in a keen high shriek that apparently went through the roof of the church and into the very treetops outside. The performance equaled anything that had been expected, "and then some."

Sister Sary-Ann Davis must have been physically exhausted, but she sank into her seat with a glad look upon her face, as though to say, "I knew I could do it." After that there was a lull in which people looked at each other with questioning glances, but said nothing.

From the next class there stepped forth as a soloist a small dark-eyed woman, probably twenty-five or thirty years old, a woman with a sweet face and gentle manner. She had a clear mezzo-soprano voice, and sang with much feeling and understanding that old favorite, Rock of Ages. A hush fell upon the congregation while she sang. This concluded the contest. The people rose to their feet and joined the leader in one great concert of religious feeling, "How Firm a Foundation." Then the judges retired for a few minutes, returned and announced the awards. That for the women went to the last singer, Sister Frances Lewis.

## 20

### THE BACKWOODS PARTY

In retrospect let us attend a Backwoods party of the long ago. It was to be at the home of Mr. and Mrs. Tom Kennedy, generally best-loved elderly couple in Canoochee Backwoods. The party was an annual affair, a harvest rejoicing that ushered in the series of frolics which extended from the early fall through the Christmas Holidays. The date had been announced, and all the younger element, at least, of Old Canoochee was in a state of bustle and glad excitement.

Mr. and Mrs. Kennedy, familiarly and affectionately known as Uncle Tom and Mis' Polly Tom, who were as much interested as the boys and girls because of the coming event, had not forgotten that they had been young once and had loved to frolic. They took part in most of the neighborhood festivities, and were always ready to open their home to the young people.

One elderly critic, referred to behind his back as "Old Sour Face," had from time to time declared that "the way that Tom and Polly Tom Kannady cut up along with the young folks was puffecly scanalous"; and once he stated, "I hyur that Tom Kannady danced the 'Fisher's Hornpipe' for the young folks at the party t'other night. Now, Whadda ya think o' that? What's this settlement a comin' to? Why, me an' Tom Kannady was boys tergether." That was the rub, perhaps. Sour Face had rheumatism and felt his age, while Uncle was considered spry for his years.

Uncle and Mis' Polly Tom didn't mind the criticism since they felt that they were right. "It was better to make people happy than not; an' they was no mo' harm in dancin' an' kissin' plays than when they was young." Uncle Tom had been a great dancer in his youth, and was not averse to shaking his foot now when occasion offered. Mis' Polly Tom could not join because of rheumatism, but she did enjoy watching the others, and from the side lines could sing the same old singing plays they had sung when she was a girl— "Green Grow the Rushes," and others.

The Kennedy's big double-pen loghouse, with its hallway, broad piazzas, front and back, the "shed rooms" for dressing, was the best adapted for a party of any in Canoochee Backwoods. It afforded ample room for the square dances and the singing plays.

In advance of the party, committees of arrangement had been appointed. As a party was a frequently recurring affair in the season, the term of each committee lasted through several months. Girls and young men went to the Kennedy home and set everything in order. The house was scrubbed, swept and garnished in the very best manner. The boys hauled the lightwood for the firestands. These last were tableshaped platforms about four feet high and three feet across, which had been thickly covered with earth, or clay and sand. On these platforms, one on each side of the front gate, fires were lighted at night. The cheery blaze sent forth brightened the whole premises and sent an inviting glow to the road beyond. The young men also brought green boughs and Spanish moss which they festooned over doors and windows—and when the committee left, Mis' Polly Tom's "house wore a very festive air." Next day after the party, the committee returned and restored everything to the usual order.

Girls and women were at home cooking for the party nearly the whole day. Young people, especially, have healthy, growing appetites and there must be an abundance for all. Besides, the opportunity of exhibiting her housewifely skill as a cook was not to be lost sight of by any girl. The rivalry between the girls was generally friendly, but no one was foolish enough to be "cut out" by even her best friend. The young people were so well acquainted that each of the girls had learned the preferences of different young men for certain viands; and each girl had the artfulness and tact to make known to her favorite young man that a certain thing which he liked had been prepared by her.

Some days before the cooking began, there had been much inspection of wardrobes, the furbishing of party dresses, probably the adding of new ribbons to freshen the appearance of an old dress. These had been bought with their own individual money at the nearby country store. In the domestic economy of Benton Center, girls, as well as boys, had an opportunity to make their spending money, over which they had complete control. That money was earned in various ways. The boys would have a pig ("shote"), or a calf that they could trade. Perhaps the father, if he was a just and kind-hearted man, would reward the boys for some special or overtime work on the farm. The girls might raise their own flock of chickens or turkeys; maybe the mother would divide the butter money with them. In these ways the youngsters acquired habits of thrift and independence which stood them in good stead later on. But, let's go to the party.

An indispensable possession for any young man "goin' a courtin'" was a two-seated buggy and a lively fast-trotting horse. It was a great advantage if the horse was known for both speed and style. All the courtin' couples went to the party in their own conveyance, and let it be known that there were times when "Two's company, three's trumpery." Every marriageable girl, of course, liked the distinction of riding alone with one of the goodlooking eligible young men; and to win that distinction made herself as pretty and attractive as possible. Rouge was taboo in those days except among faded society ladies, none of whom lived in Benton Center. It is a trite aphorism that "Beauty when unadorned is most adorned." The girls of Benton Center were not lacking in natural charms—clear, healthy complexion, bright eyes, gleaming teeth, and a wealth of pretty hair, a supple well-rounded form, an a quick, light and graceful step. A peculiar charm of the girls of Benton Center was a modest demeanor and a sweet seriousness of manner. The young men were a fine, upstanding lot. Clean, open air living, manly courage, a sense of personal responsibility in their business and social relations, and a steadfast purpose in life, were their shining virtues. There were probably some who did not reach a high standard, but they were in the minority. Benton Center demanded of its men certain rules of decent living to which they had to conform if they had any worthwhile rating in the community.

The courtin' couples having sped away toward the scene of the party (they were supposed to take the longest way round, so they started early), others in large numbers were soon wending their way in the direction of the Kennedy home. There were no automobiles in those days to raise the question of convenient parking places, but the horses and vehicles had to be cared for. Most families had only one or two hitching posts before the front door, but Uncle Tom had a long horizontal bar erected at one side of the front where twenty or more horses could be tethered by the bridle, and space found for all the vehicles—buggies and farm wagons. A few of the younger boys rode horseback and those who lived near walked. But it was considered bad form for a man of the dancing set to ride horseback alone. Some of the girls came with brothers and younger sisters, but otherwise they had escorts of their own.

It is a well-known fact that the upper and the under crusts of society engage most in pleasure, the former to get rid of ennui (and their money, perhaps), the latter because of the zest for living, the natural craving for amusement. Each class has to adapt itself to local conditions, and "Evil be to him who evil thinks of it" may be applied anywhere.

In Savannah, the Coast town, the society folk danced the Cotillion and the stately Minuet—the same kind of dances that had been known to the society of powdered wigs, the patches and rouge of an earlier time. New dances from the Old World were coming into favor in the upper society—the Schottische, the Polka, and the beautiful waltz for which the most sensuous and entrancing music was written. Pastimes in the backwoods were just as enjoyable, perhaps more so to the participants, but there was less restraint and more vigor thrown into them. Though less refined in a way, the backwoods pleasures were just as innocent—the very spontaneous expression of happy youth.

When all the guests had arrived at the Kennedy home, and the fiddlers were in readiness, festivities began. The initiation came with that time-honored and exhilarating tune, "Turkey in the straw," than which a more enlivening combinations of musical sounds was never written. It is challenged that no one of any animation, hearing that tune played with the gusto of an old time fiddler, can keep the feet still or the body in repose. The dances were the square dances. The figures were called in a loud stentorian voice to the accompaniment of a pounding foot. The same man had called the figures for many years and was considered an expert.

Came the command, "Find Yore Pardners," "All Promenade," and they promenaded to appropriate measure, the music changing and fitting in, "Take Yore Places." This led to a lively scramble. Some of the couples had been arranged in advance, but there was frequently a timid youth who had to wait until the last minute to get up his courage to ask the girl of his choice to join him, and that being possible only through fear that some rival would get ahead of him. Then, "Salute Yore Pardners," "Balance All," "Cross Over, Ladies to the Right, Gentlemen to the Left," "Back Agin, Ladies to the Left, Gentlemen to the Right," "Swing Yore Pardners," "Sasshay (Chassez) All," (Here a lively gallop ensued), "Take Yore Places," "Hands Across," "First Couple Down the Aisle and Back Agin," "Second Couple," (This included in succession one half the couples, when the order of "Down the Aisle and Back Agin" was reversed). "Turn," "Break."

There were two sets in the hallway and one set on the big wide piazza. Dancing was continued until all who wished had had a part. Dancing was followed by an old folk-play. This game seemed so familiar and well understood that it was conducted in regular sequence and with no further prompting than "Find Yore Pardners." A gentleman approached his lady partner, and holding out his right hand sings or says, "I give my right hand a shake, shake, shake, and I turn my partner round." This was followed by suitable gestures. Then, "I give my left hand a shake, shake, shake, and I turn my partner round." And so on with the right foot and the left foot, the movements toward the left reversing the right. There was then much "turning" right and left.

There was a game of forfeits and with the redeeming of the pledges much open kissing and measuring of "yards of love ribbon." A boy and a girl standing opposite, holding hands and reaching right and left and lightly kissing, each time marked the supposed number of "yards." This game in its procedure was openly approved by their elders as being quite proper. Then followed more singing plays, "Green Grow the Rushes," and others as time honored. "Stealing Partners" was a lively game: "You Steal My True Love, I steal Her Back Again, Green Grows the Willow Tree."

The conclusion of the next game marked the time for supper. Girls and young men were ranged on opposite sides, each girl representing some lovely flower. Others then sang to the young men in turn, "There's a Rose in the garden for you, Young Man, a Rose (or a Lily) for you." The young man so addressed stepped forth, acknowledged the message and turned to one of the girls waiting for him on the opposite side, either singing or saying, "I seek and I find" and as he approached the girl, "Fair Lady, give me your lily-white hand and take a walk with me." After these little dramatics (so like Comic Opera), and the roses and lilies and daffy-down-dillies were all paired off and holding hands, supper was announced in a way that all may hear. Other partnerships were speedily formed and there was a mild rush to the supper tables.

The sight of those tables would have delighted the eyes of any epicure. There were three of them, set in one of the big rooms and literally loaded with nearly every choice edible known to Benton housewives. There was much variety because the food had come from different families and you could take your choice. Roast pork, roast beef, boiled ham (home-cured), roast and fried chicken, chicken pilau, great quantities of homemade lightbread and rich creamy butter, delicious biscuit (made with "saleratus" and sour milk), sweet potato "pone," sweet potato pie, homedried peach and apple pie, pickles, pound cake. To top off all this, plenty of black coffee with great jugs of sweet rich cream and homemade light brown "coffee sugar." There was no stint of anything.

Several matrons of the neighborhood assisted the committee in the serving. Uncle Tom and Miss Polly Tom had special attention. Back in the kitchen where the coffee was made, a basket of the choicest of everything had been set aside in advance for the elderly couple. One thoughtful woman remarked that Mis' Polly Tom would not have to cook much for some days. Uncle Tom was a wise man in his day and time. With the aid of the committee he had made sure that no contraband liquor had been hidden away; and everybody stayed sober. After the supper was over, came "The Irish Trot." They formed a large ring, then turned in opposite directions, one-half going, and the other half coming. There was much catching and releasing of hands, much turning and twisting as they "trotted" and lustily sang:

> "Hands all around in the Irish Trot,
> Hands all around in the Irish Trot,
> Heigho, Heigho, Heigho,
> Way down below."

This was a rollicking game and quite boisterous enough to please the junior boys and girls who had come with older brothers and sisters. Then followed other singing plays and more dancing. Dancing was not looked upon with the disfavor as shown in some communities. Their ancestors had danced and the custom had been handed down in good repute with others that still prevailed. The Irish Jig, The Sailor's Hornpipe, The Highland Fling, The Scottish Reel, were not forgotten. Frequently some man who had been taught by his father would give an exhibition of his agility by dancing for the company one of those dances his ancestors had danced in the old British homeland.

The party came to an end with a modification of the old Sir Roger de Coverly, or as better known locally, The Virginia Reel. Tired and happy, the revelers went home in the beautiful light of the golden harvest moon. To them all the world was young.

*[Concluded.]*

The Cracker cart was a common site in the Ogeechee-Canoochee backwoods. Julia Harn describes it as follows: "One unique type of vehicle was the Cracker cart, popular with the small farmers because of its cheapness and its adaptability to varied uses, and its durability. The cart was often used as the family carriage, even to town, and for hauling small loads about the farm. It was built by the local blacksmith and wheelwright. The original idea of the Cracker cart may have been borrowed from the Spanish settlers in Florida." (Courtesy of Special Collections, Lucile Hodges Papers, Zack Henderson Library, Georgia Southern University.)

# Appendix One

## *List of Julia Harn's Articles Published in the Georgia Historical Quarterly*

## *Georgia Historical Quarterly*
## Julia Harn Articles

### *Old Canoochee-Ogeechee Chronicles*

### *Old Canoochee Backwoods Sketches*

X. The Wayfarer, Sugar Cane, Sowing and Reaping, Vol. 24, No. 2, June 1940, p. 158-162.

XI. Gardening, Food Conservation, Poultry, Vol. 24, No. 3, September 1940, p. 272-277.

XII. Cattle, Vol. 24, No. 4, December 1940, p. 382-385.

XIII. Houses, Vol. 25, No. 1, March 1941, p. 77-79.

XIV. Outdoor Sports, Goin' to Town, The All-Day Sing, Vol. 25, No. 2, June 1941, p. 172-180.

XV. The Backwoods Party, Vol. 41, no. 3, September 1941, p. 286-291.

Note: Roman numerals used to correspond with articles as published in the *Georgia Historical Quarterly*.

# Appendix Two

*Colonial Harn Family Sketch*
*by Julia Harn*

# HARN FAMILY
## COLONIAL SKETCH

John Harn, the original Scotch settler, (or "immigrant" as then known), came from Scotland to South Carolina, thence to Bryan County, (St. Philips Parish), Georgia accompanied by his five brothers, his family of wife, nine sons and daughters, and twenty-nine indentured servants, sometime in the 1740s. John Harn settled in the peninsula known as Bryan Neck and was granted Dublin or Richmond Plantation. He later removed to the lower Canoochee River Valley, not far from its confluence with the Great Ogeechee River. This plantation developed, and became the permanent home of the family. In fact, the property remained the possession of the Harn family for more than a hundred years.

This Canoochee Plantation was a magnificent estate, extending for several miles along one bank of the Canoochee River. Because of the indentured servants John Harn was able to secure larger grants of land: moreover, this section held many advantages: great forests of the finest timber, fertile soil, and water transportation. By the nearest land route Savannah was less than twenty-five miles away. Timber and heavy farm products could be sent by raft and barge to the mouth of the Great Ogeechee River, and thence between the Sea Islands up the coast to the city market in Savannah.

The ban against African Slavery so rigidly maintained in the time of Oglethorpe and for some years after, was lifted in 1750. The introduction of Negro slaves brought about many changes in the industrial and economic life of the Colony of Georgia. Many of the more enterprising of the indentured servants secured land and were encouraged to become independent and respected citizens.

Georgia having been the last settled of the original Thirteen Colonies held many British sympathizers during the Revolutionary War. Dating from the close of the Seven Years War in Europe in 1763, until the close of the Revolution in America in 1783, Florida was in possession of the British, known as "Tories" and thoroughly detested. The British committed many depredations upon the lives and property of the American Patriots, besides instigating the

Indians to acts of violence upon the sparsely settled communities of the neighboring whites. John Harn, the Scotch settler, became an ardent American patriot. Two of his sons William and Thomas, were Revolutionary soldiers and his home and his purse strings were open to any wounded Continental soldier.

John Harn was a member of the First Colonial Assembly of Georgia in 1755 but he was not permitted to finish out the term. He and seven of his colleagues were tried for sedition and expelled. Those were troublous times. Seeds of revolution against the British Government and more particularly against the King George III, were being sown in various sections of the Colonies. John Harn and his seven colleagues were proven of having sent the following revolutionary letter to the more influential men of the surrounding plantations:

"Savannah, 15th January, 1755 - - - Gentlemen: If you regard the libertys of your country, and we cannot doubt they are dear to you, it is highly necessary that you come immediately to Savannah, there by your presence to animate and support your friends in the endeavors to procure those blessings that can alone render this Colony flourishing and happy.

In this hope we will not fail, and subscribe ourselves hearty and sincere friends of Georgia.

(signed)

| | |
|---|---|
| Charles Watson | John Farmer |
| Mark Carr | John Harn |
| Edmond Gray | John Mackintosh |
| William Gray | Edward Barnard |

To the freeholders of the Province of Georgia"

The letter having been intercepted and falling into the hands of the royal Governor Reynolds, drastic action was taken and the eight members of the House of Representatives were expelled.

The Scotch-American gentleman John Harn seems to have been a man of affairs and progressive tendencies. He left his impress upon the community and the section of the State where he lived, and inspired his children with an ardent love for the new homeland. To his descendants he bequeathed an honorable name, and an extensive landed estate that was a rural paradise, deep forest, broad fields, and pasture lands with herds of cattle and a comfortable home where the wayfarer as well as the invited guest could find a resting place. The location was ideal upon an inland waterway that led down to the sea not many miles afar.

Not all of the Harn family (clan) who came from Scotland to America settled in the southeast. Some of them landed on the Eastern Shore of Maryland, moved down to the Carolinas, then migrated westward where their descendants are today, having spread into Texas, Louisiana, into Ohio and other Midwestern States. So far as known, many or all of them maintain the inherent characteristics of pride, and a spirit of sturdy independence.

Julia Harn

Source: University of Florida George A. Smathers Libraries, Julia A. Harn Manuscripts, MS 73.

# Appendix Three

## *Civil War Service of Julia Harn's Father, Samuel Harn, as Commissary Agent*

# SAMUEL HARN IN THE CIVIL WAR

The enclosed sketch of the war services of my father, Samuel Harn during the War Between the States is copied from what my father told me and asked me to write down for him (perhaps because he knew that I wanted it [to join the United Daughters of the Confederacy, ed.]) sometime in the year of 1900, in Savannah, Georgia. My father died in Savannah, March 11, 1901.

Very much of what is contained in this sketch I know of and do distinctly remember. In the year 1925/6, I had in my possession a large pair of steel shears that were used in cutting apart the sheets or bills of Confederate money which my father's sketch tells about. That money was closely guarded and my mother and her sister Mrs. Hall (afterwards Mrs. Messick) did the cutting and I was permitted to look on. I remember that this money was tacked between towels or pieces of cloth and that my father and his body servant wore those packs on their backs when they left home. Therein lay an element of danger that my father bravely faced along with other duties.

Julia Harn

Gainesville, Fla.,
Feb. 16, 1932

Note: My father did not sign this sketch because he was then blind from cataracts in both eyes. The cataracts were later removed shortly before he died in 1901 at Savannah, Georgia and he is buried in our lot in Laurel Grove Cemetery there.

Samuel Harn

Born in Bryan County, Georgia, July 2, 1826.
At the breaking out of the hostilities between the North and South, I was sworn in under ___ Brown, (brother of Governor Joseph E. Brown) and General Whitaker at Savannah, to act under orders from Major Joseph Locke, N.E. Solomons, and Major J.L. Villalonga, as a quartermaster, my duties being to supply the Georgia

State troops with meat in the way of beef and bacon, to buy and ship to various points livestock (cattle), and bacon as needed.

When the Confederate Government superseded the State in authority, I was then appointed by the late McPherson B. Millen and those first named to travel and buy supplies in the way of cattle, hogs, sugar, syrup, and bacon, with orders to purchase corn when necessary and have the animals fattened. My territory included the states of Georgia, Florida, South Carolina, North Carolina, Tennessee, and Kentucky.

I was given the right to name and appoint agents under me in that territory, and to detail men, soldiers form any regiment, wherever needed, the number of these last not to exceed thirty-two, to assist in the work of herding and driving the livestock. I had stock pens at many places in the states traveled.

At first I appointed two men, by name Somers and Gardner, for Kentucky, J.O. Hicks and James Hicks for Tennessee, and McConnell for North Carolina, reserving for my own territory the States of Georgia, South Carolina, and Florida. These sub-agents traveling shipped many thousands of cattle to me directly at Savannah. From this point I shipped to various other places wherever needed. After the fighting in the upper part of my territory became so sharp and continuos, I gave up that part and confined my work to Georgia and Florida.

I established a stock pen at Scarboro, Ga., Central Rail Road, for hogs. In the aggregate the hogs shipped there numbered forty thousand or more. There were many shipping points in this state for the cattle. I shipped to the late Wm. H. Davis of Savannah in all many thousands of cattle to be slaughtered here for the soldiers. There were other agents of the Confederate Government traveling in the same capacity as myself, and in the same territory, whose duty it was to assist each other as much as possible.

In addition to buying for the Confederate soldiers, the state of Georgia, about 1863, if I remember right, attempted to provide until the end of the war for the indigent women and children of the state. I had to purchase supplies for them to be shipped to various points for distribution. For the faithful performance of this work, I gave bond in the sum of $40,000 to the state of Georgia, Joseph E. Brown, Governor. My sureties were A.T. McIntire, A. P. Wright, and James L.

Seward of Thomasville, Georgia. I continued my work under both commissions until the close of the war, and continued it until my commission was destroyed by the Yankees, and the Confederacy had fallen.

My traveling expenses were paid by the Government, but I furnished my own horses and also two of my own men slaves to help me. For the last two years I drew no pay for these services other than the traveling expenses. For rail road fare, I was empowered to write my own tickets, could order trains of cars to take supplies whenever and wherever needed, the military authority being above the civil. The purchase money for the livestock and other supplies I drew from the Government upon my order countersigned by Major Millen. I returned vouchers to headquarters for all purchases made, and gave a full account of every transaction. It may be noted in passing, that the amount of Confederate money drawn at any one time usually was from $50,000 to $100,000, perhaps the largest sum at any one time was $150,000.

As above stated, I continued this business until the close of the War; many times risking my life in the discharge of duty, since it was often necessary to go into remote country districts particularly in Florida, where there were many deserters and outlaws in the swamps, and others who resented the wholesale selling of their livestock to the Confederate Government for the paper money I paid them. Twice I was captured by the enemy near the close of the war, and released again within a short time.

Once (March 1862) I contracted a very serious illness, typhoid, and was ill for many weeks in Savannah, part of which time I was attended by the late Dr. James Schley, Sr. Twice when the call for soldiers became urgent I was exempt from military duty, because my services were deemed more valuable in the capacity in which I was then acting than as a regular solder.

Having passed through the many experiences, herein but briefly outlined, I feel that I am in name and in truth.

A Confederate Veteran.

Source: University of Florida George A. Smathers Libraries, Julia A. Harn, Manuscripts, MS 73.

# Index

Note: Numbers in italics indicate illustrations.

ABOUT THE COMPILER

Pharris Johnson's interest in local history led him to write five previous books on the subject. These include *Evans County and the Creation of Ft. Stewart, Georgia; Under the Southern Cross – Soldier Life with Gordon Bradwell and the Army of Northern Virginia; Bellville, Georgia, The First Hundred Years; Houses of Heart Pine – A Survey of the Antebellum Architecture of Evans County, Georgia;* and *Tattnall County Deed Book D-E-F.* He also co-authored *Images of America: Evans County.*

Johnson served in the Air Force as a colonel and held logistics positions at base, headquarters, and Defense Logistics Agency levels during his 28-year military career. After he retired from the Air Force, Johnson served in leadership roles with the Savannah College of Art and Design at both the Savannah and Atlanta campuses.

Johnson and his wife, Annie, live in Bellville, Georgia, where he was elected mayor in 2016.

Made in the USA
Columbia, SC
10 November 2022

70884685R00104